When Love Isn't Enough: A guide for dog fosters, rescues and owners.

Nikki Ivey

Copyright © 2013 Nikki Ivey/DogSpeak

All rights reserved.

ISBN-13: **978-1484142394**

DEDICATION

I dedicate this book to all the dog rescuers, fosters and owners that have spent years loving dogs that no one else loved. Your passion, desire and strength are a gift from God. You have shown me that only angels can do what you do. I pray this book becomes a 'go-to' guide for you as you spend countless hours nursing back sick dogs, rehabilitating dogs with serious behavior issues or housetraining the litter of eight.

CONTENTS

	Acknowledgments	I
	Introduction	8
1	The Business of Rescue	11
2	Should You Foster?	20
3	Dogs' Needs	28
4	Dog Communication and Language	40
5	Setting Expectations	52
6	Basics of Training	55
7	Use of Training Tools	65
8	Real Life Manners	73
9	Common Puppy Problems	122
10.	Behavior Problems	135
11.	Being in Public and Extra Activities	161
12.	Resources	169
	About the Author	170

ACKNOWLEDGMENTS

I'm so grateful for the gift that God has given me and the knowledge to put together this book for those that love dogs like I do. I'm blessed every day I get to change someone's thought process and bring them just a step closer to truly understanding God's gift to man, the dog. I pray that I will always remain on His path and that each day I have the opportunity to change a dog's life through humans.

This book has been in the works for many years but it wasn't until God put the right two people in my life that it truly came to fruition. I must thank my dear friends, and editors, Cynthia Avery and Britteny Watson, for the long hours they put in making my words flow perfectly on these pages. I couldn't do it without you and I'm so grateful you two are in my life.

Lastly, I want to thank Britteny Watson of Compactio Marketing, for the amazing job she's done putting DogSpeak™ on the map. My business grows every day because of her dedication and hard work. Thank you for being my manager, marketing director and, most importantly, my friend.

INTRODUCTION

Every year thousands of dogs are rescued from the streets, abusive homes, and from puppy mills. Consequently, the burden falls on non-profit organizations to rescue these unwanted, abused and neglected canines and help them find forever homes. If you are reading this book, it probably means that you are one of those dedicated individuals who either runs a rescue or volunteers at one.

In my experience as a dog behavior consultant and trainer for rescue organizations I have found that many volunteers experience moments of burnout due to spending their own money, getting emotionally attached to their foster, not being able to manage an uncontrollable dog, and the feeling of failure when a dog is returned to the shelter or, sadly euthanized.
This book will provide valuable, eye-opening information that will change the way you rescue dogs. -Adopting the guidelines on the following pages will change the way you think, feel and interact with the dogs that you foster and with your rescue organization. I guarantee that you will see positive results and by the end of this book officially be a "DogSpeak™ geek"

A SPECIAL ACKNOWLEDGEMENT

Before I go any farther, I wish to acknowledge the commitment it takes to be in the rescue world. Not everyone is capable of working with rescues or volunteering in shelters. I believe it takes special angels to do this work and I praise each and every one of you for your effort.

I have consulted with animal shelters, rescue organizations and foster volunteers for over a decade and have found that their major problem was love. Yes, Love. Love was doled out in buckets without it being anchored to a proven training foundation. It was like seeing someone trying to use an awesome tool without the knowledge to turn it on. The volunteers felt love, but that love clouded their judgment and prevented them from fully educating themselves. This made their efforts futile. I knew that with the right amount of DogSpeak education, coupled with their unending passion, these volunteers could make a monumental difference in the lives of these fragile dogs.

So, in 2009, I put together a presentation for fosters, rescues, shelters and animal control agencies called, "When Love Isn't Enough," With the help of the Mars Corporation, I brought the DogSpeak training method to one hundred volunteers and professionals. Since that first seminar, the DogSpeak method has been presented over twenty more times to countless passionate rescue volunteers, like yourself. After each seminar, I received endless feedback, testimonials and requests for printed instruction in this proven method. It was then, that I realized the need for this book.

My hope for you, by the end of this book, is that you will see that a well-socialized, self-controlled and confident dog is a happy dog; one that is adoptable and one that is, forever loved. May God bless your role as a rescuer of dogs!

Nikki Ivey
Professional Trainer/Behavior Consultant
DogSpeak

CHAPTER 1
THE BUSINESS OF RESCUE

Many rescue organizations get overwhelmed not long after the "Open" sign is hung on the door. When I ask founders of non-profit rescues, "Why did you become a rescue organization?" I receive two common answers; "We saw a need," and "We love dogs." However, I have found that these well-meaning individuals fail to see beyond the passion and beyond the need. They fail to see the business aspect of their altruistic endeavor. Sadly, the business consulting component of DogSpeak is usually utilized after these floundering organizations find themselves entangled in an over-burdened mission, a lack of essential resources, and inefficient tools to manage their clients; that being abandoned, neglected and abused dogs.

A second question that I ask founders of non-profit rescue organizations is, "How do you measure success?" They summarily answer, "With the number of adoptions we have every year!" Adoptions are a very important aspect of a rescue's mission, but the number of adoptions is not a complete and true measure of success. Ultimately, success is measured in the quality of the product that the organization is able to deliver. A rescue organization needs to conduct a thorough self-analysis as to what product it can deliver at the level and structure they are at. The organization needs to evaluate the skills and abilities of its employees and volunteers. It needs to assess its resources and be realistic as to the number of dogs it can save and not take on the burden of the ones it can't. An organization that has realistic goals, solid procedures, and functions within its limitations will prosper and rehome more dogs than one that operate under an overzealous, misdirected, unsystematic crisis management business model.

Whether you are a non-profit rescue organization or a publicly funded shelter, I encourage you to enlist the services of a professional consultant in building your rescue. These consultants help organizations succeed by strengthening small business and non-profit's management structure and offering solutions to issues facing the small business and non-profit community.

The Measure of Success:
Rescuing and Pulling the Right Dog

Take a tour of any shelter. You will find many of the dogs were relinquished or abandoned due to behavior issues that could have been corrected, such as chewing, jumping, barking and nipping. These dogs were not bad, they were just owned by uneducated humans. To educate the entire population of potential dog owners is a grandiose goal, and especially not one attainable for a small, non-profit rescue organization. Therefore, the goal must be redirected toward producing a well-mannered, good-tempered adoptable dog. The goal should not be to rescue a dog that taxes the organization's resources, exhausts the volunteer's time and emotions and that has a low probability of adoption. You do not want to waste resources that could be used on a more viable dog. The goal is to keep more dogs in their homes and decrease the number of dogs that end up in shelters.

As hard as it is to hear, not every dog without a home is adoptable. Some dogs have serious and potentially dangerous, behavior issues. Others have health issues that, although expensive medical procedures may extend their life by weeks, it will put your organization in the red for months. I wish there were homes for every dog in this world, but in reality, there is not. The sooner you realize this the sooner you will be more successful in adopting out your rescued dogs.

Rescuing

If you have implemented a rescue division as part of your organizational structure (as opposed to pulling prospective dogs from shelters), then you should have also set aside funds for the initial medical care and behavioral assessment of the dog that was rescued. If you did not, then you should not be rescuing dogs. Leave that function to organizations that prioritize their resources to handle this difficult and expensive task. Nevertheless, it is beneficial to network with and develop a good working relationship with rescue organizations and animal control agencies so that if you find yourself in a rescue predicament, you can turn the matter over to individuals who have the experience and funds to handle the situation.

Knowing what your organization can do and, more importantly, what your organization cannot do will bring you closer to your definition of success.

Rescuing dogs from the community can be burdensome on an organization. That is why many elect to pull dogs that have already been turned over to a shelter. This allows for a more controlled assessment and evaluation of the dog for foster care, training and ultimately adoption. But, certainly there is a need for on-site rescue. The key to on-site rescue is that you have protocols that guide your rescuers legally, morally and ethically.

Pulling

When you walk into a shelter to pull dogs for your rescue organization, you know going in, that you cannot take them all; so how do you know which ones to pull? It is established that you love dogs, but love is not enough. There are puppies, young dogs, adult dogs and senior dogs. There are mixed breeds, pedigrees, cute dogs and ugly dogs. Do you take a frisky puppy over a well-mannered senior dog? Do you take a dog that barks out of fear or one that cringes in the back of a kennel? It has been said that black dogs do not get adopted as quickly as the lighter colored ones, but what are the real attributes that you must look at to know if a dog is adoptable?

First, look at your fosters with clear eyes. You must know the limitations and abilities of each foster registered with your organization. Pulling dogs that have issues without fosters that can handle them is a mistake organizations regularly make. Each foster should only have one foster dog at a time. Ideally, you want to see a rescue enter the foster home and be adopted within six weeks. I recommend that each foster get, at least, one-week break between rescues to avoid burnout. You will want to choose dogs that will flourish in your group of fosters. Choosing the right dog will help you increase your adoption success, and subsequently increase your rescue numbers.

Many dogs that enter shelters have behavior issues. The most common is fear and anxiety. These dogs are desperate for someone to build their confidence and help them overcome the issues that plague them. It takes a trained eye and a good temperament test to determine whether the behavior of the dog can be corrected with the proper foster care and training. Many incorrigible behaviors can be corrected and others cannot. Focus on the dogs that you can save, rehabilitate and find a forever home. The dog in the shelter with heartworms may not be the right rescue to take in, nor is the one that will not stop chasing its tail. If your organization does not have the resources to treat these disorders, then you must move on.

Next, it is a good idea to know the history behind the dog in the shelter. If it is not listed on the kennel card, then make an inquiry with the shelter intake personnel. A particular dog's behavior may be a result of an abusive past. This history will aid in determining whether the dog can be rehabilitated. For instance, a chained dog is different than the stray dog that has been around other dogs, cats, children and adults. The chained dog may have only been exposed to his owner and a neighbor dog that comes and steals his food. An investigation as to how and why this dog came into the shelter will provide crucial information as to the probability of rehabilitation and integration into a more socialized setting. Another example would be to enquire as to the scars on a dog. Was the dog used for fighting, was it beaten, or a stray used to fending for itself? Or, was it once someone's pet that lost its way? Due diligence into the prospective rescue's past can pay in the end.

Lastly, have an idea of what people are looking for in your area. Every person is looking for a different size, personality, energy level and look, but there should be some common attributes that are common for your community. Individuals who live in a rural area where there is hunting and farms and livestock will be looking for different dogs than individuals who live in an urban area with single family homes and an abundance of schools and parks. These inquiries may be centered around young dogs, medium in size and good with children. Only you will know what your community is looking for.

Take the time to educate yourself on the needs of your community, the knowledge of your resources and what you can realistically do. Be careful when choosing which dogs to bring into your organization. Feel good for the ones that you can help and do not focus on feeling bad for the ones that you cannot. There are many organizations rescuing dogs, so stop trying to do it all yourself. Reach out to other local groups and band together as a unit and you will be amazed at the progress you can make.

Adoption

Once your rescue is ready for placement, the next step is to find his forever home. Your organization could have the best rescue model on the books, but if you do not place the right rescue with the right adopted home, then your work was all for naught. Currently, the most popular way to promote adoptable pets is via the Internet. Make use of social media sites and create a professional, informative and easy to navigate website. Be advised that with unsanitary hoarding cases proliferating and puppy mills being exposed, adopters are more wary about where they get their dog. The last thing you want to do is scare potential adopters toward a pet store that could actually be purchasing their stock from an unsavory puppy mill.

If you continue to develop a trusting relationship with other credible rescues and shelters, then networking can be a valuable tool. Relationships with other dependable individuals in the field can bring you trustworthy adopters that may have already been through one or more screening processes. Never discount word of mouth referrals. A satisfied customer walking their adopted (and well mannered!) dog in a community park can do as much positive advertising as television and radio combined.

Screening potential adopters is important and it should be done thoroughly and systematically. If you carefully screen your potential adopters and ensure they adopt the appropriate dog, then the possibility of a return drops dramatically.

Although the task of developing standard screening protocol is daunting, it is obviously necessary. I understand that it is difficult to put together a list to help you match the right dog with the right family or individual. Nevertheless, knowing how to match a dog's breed, individual personality and temperament with a prospective adopter is as good as gold. Thus, the screening and placement volunteer should be trained, not only in reading an adopters placement potential, but how to ask the right questions tailored toward educating the adopter as to what dog would be right for him or her, or their growing family. The movie 101 Dalmatians did more than promote the spotted breed. It placed 1001 Dalmatians into rescues across the country. Cute does not always cut it.

Finally, the last and often over looked component of a successful rescue organization is the post adoption follow-up. A top attribute of any business is customer service. That means that you not only give great customer service prior to the transaction, but also during and after the transaction. Especially when the transaction deals with a living and breathing purchase. Having contact with fosters post adoption is crucial to your organization.

Post Adoption

New adopters are usually thrilled with their recent and "adorable" addition to the family. That is, until the honeymoon is over. This "grace period" usually lasts two weeks and then reality sets in. Both dog and human move past getting acquainted and they begin to view each other differently. The cute puppy that played with the slipper has now become the dog that chewed a $100.00 loafer. Most are correctable behaviors as long as the adopter realizes that these behaviors can be corrected with consistent expectations established within the household. Grace periods can be the death of a harmonious relationship between a newly adopted dog and his new owners. To assist with the fallout, your organization should prepare the new owners regarding the "grace period" phenomena and then, have someone follow up each week, for the first month. Doing this will allow the adopter to ask questions that may arise and in turn, it will allow you to assist with minor adjustments or allow you to refer the new adopted family to a reputable behaviorist or professional trainer.

CHAPTER 2
SHOULD YOU FOSTER?

Being a dog foster requires more than offering love and shelter to a dog in need. Whether you are thinking of being a foster or are already one but are overwhelmed, you should ask yourself some serious questions before continuing:

Why do I want to foster dogs?

Do I have control of my own dogs?

Do I have the support of my family or roommates?

Do I have the time and money to invest in a foster dog?

Why Do I Want to Foster Dogs?

When I ask this question, I always get the same answer: because you love dogs. This is evident by your decision to take on this challenge. However, there is more to fostering than just offering love. It is important you implement discipline and expectations when dealing with fosters so as to avoid creating new issues or making existing issues worse. Successful businesses and non-profits need to run from a state of sound reason as opposed to emotion. Hence, the reason for a diverse non-profit board of directors. Their job is to look at their organization from a rational point-of-view through the lens of their expertise. Emotions are reactive as opposed to proactive. As a foster, you must act with rationale rather than emotion. Being emotional will often cause you to give in to bad behavior. As humans, we tend to baby and coddle dogs when they are exhibiting bad behavior. We also make excuses for their behavior. While past trauma can cause a dog to act or behave a certain way, we must not allow a dog's past to dictate how we treat them going forward. As a strong leader, it is your responsibility to show compassion without allowing bad behavior, phobias and fears to worsen. Here is your first lesson: *Reactive human emotion reinforces fear within a dog.*

Many dog owners think of their four-legged creatures as children. As someone without children, I can empathize with this sentiment. Again, forgetting that dogs are not human can cause more harm than good. Dogs can be our best friends, our confidants, the shoulders on which we cry, and our running buddies. They are amazing animals that love us no matter. For me, dogs are my livelihood, co-workers, and passion. They have taught me patience as well as how to communicate and teach. However, because we often respond to dogs' behavior sympathetically and anthropomorphically, we again reinforce fears and unwanted behaviors. We do this when we baby, coddle, soothe and comfort, which is great for humans but dangerous for dogs.

Dogs have different needs than two-legged children.

Children can rationalize and understand when they are being protected and consoled. Dogs see any sort of consolation and attention as conformation that their behavior is acceptable. That is not to say that you should not or cannot love a dog. I personally feel dogs can also show love and compassion toward humans and other creatures. It is important, however, to understand dog language and communication in order to properly offer and receive this love.

Dogs need to know they can depend on you and look to you as a leader. Learning how to communicate with dogs will help you strengthen the bond you have with them. Teaching them confidence and training foundations will also allow you to build trust and love. Treats, toys and car rides are not comprehended as love, but as rewards. The same goes for coddling or soothing.

The human definition of love is what encourages you to do what you do, but the reason you foster should be because you want dogs to have the best chance possible to have their own family and the life that they deserve.

Do I Have Control of my Own Dogs?

If you have dogs that run your house, sneak out the door, jump on guests, are aggressive towards other dogs, have no leash manners or do not come when called, you do not have control of your own dogs. If you are unable to have control of your own dogs or unable to teach them appropriate manners, then you are not prepared to take in a foster that is definitely going to have issues that need to be worked on in order to be adoptable.

I encourage you to establish a strong leadership role with your own dogs and ensure that you have taught them the appropriate manners before you bring in a foster dog. Your dogs should know the rules of the house, have self-control, be well socialized and exhibit good communication skills. Your own dogs will actually play a huge mentoring role in the life of your foster if they have these attributes. This will essentially make your job as a foster much easier, and will set your foster up for success much more quickly.

Do I have the Support of My Family or Roommate?

It is extremely important that you have the support of all who live in your home. They will also be integral in the training process. They must be able to follow the rules that you implement for a dog and willing to help out when you are unable to be at home. Those that foster without the support of their family end up experiencing tension, stress and burnout much quicker than those with support. If your household is exhibiting tension and stress then you are not offering a much-needed stable environment for your foster.

I recommend sitting down with your entire household to discuss the pros and cons of bringing a foster into your home. Set expectations for each member of the household. Reiterate how important it is that you are all on the same page and that the foster dog is depending on you to get him into his forever home. This is also the time to go over the rules that you will be putting in place for the new foster. I recommend that you print the rules out and either hand them out to everyone or post them in an easily accessible place, like the refrigerator. Consider having a weekly house meeting. This will allow everyone to voice his or her concerns or progress with a foster. A weekly meeting will keep tension down and maintain a manageable level of emotion in the environment; which is critical for your foster's learning.

Do I Have the Time and Money to Invest in a Foster?

As a foster, you must invest a lot time into your foster dog. Some dogs require more time than others in order to become adoptable. For instance, a dog may need professional training. This training can range from anything to housetraining to solving behavioral issues. The time spent on the dog will depend on the extensiveness of its individual issues.

You may be responsible for writing a biography and to get great pictures to post online for potential adopters. You may also be responsible for meeting with potential adopters or attending public adoption events on a weekly basis.

In some cases, you must also be prepared to meet the financial needs of your foster. Rescue organizations typically pay for necessities such as vet care, monthly heartworm and flea prevention, and food. However, there are often other expenses an organization may not be able to cover, but that are crucial to a dog's success. These may be dog daycare, boarding, special food, treats, toys or training. I highly encourage you to put aside funds for each foster that you receive. Setting a budget will also keep the stress down for the household.

Before working with a particular rescue, inquire about what will be required of you financially.

The following are more important questions to ask yourself before you become a foster:

Do I Have the Knowledge to Train My Foster?

You do not have to be a professional dog trainer in order to teach your foster dog good manners. Every foster dog is going to have at least one bad habit or behavioral issue. It is your responsibility to extinguish that behavior and teach an appropriate one.

If you are good at the basics of housebreaking, crate training, and basic commands, then start out with dogs that need help in these areas. Try not to take on dogs that have more serious issues such as fear, anxiety and aggression until you have more experience or have the resources available to work with these issues. If you want the ability to deal with these dogs, I recommend getting as much educational experience as you can. This book will offer valuable information for laying a foundation to solve these issues, however it is important to find someone in your area who is experienced in working with serious behavior issues and uses positive techniques. Find someone who has experience working with rescues.

Will I Be Able to Part Ways When my Foster Gets Adopted?

Your goal when fostering is to find a dog a forever home. There are many foster parents who get attached to their foster and end up adopting them. Many also give up hope for finding a dog a home. I can understand getting attached or feeling that the dog is best suited for your home, but you must separate yourself from those emotions. Keep in mind that by adopting your foster, your organization may be losing a foster home. Also, if you are simply managing a dog's issues rather than correcting them, you will have less success finding a forever home for the dog, and will be more tempted to keep the dog because you feel only you can control him.

Only adopt your foster dog if you have the time and money to invest in making him a successful dog, and if you will not become overwhelmed with having too large of a pack.

So Fostering Isn't For You...Now What?

If you realize that fostering is not for you, it is okay! There are many other essential roles you can fill within a rescue organization. Rescues need transporters, fundraisers, material items, dog walkers, and monetary donations.

CHAPTER 3
DOGS' NEEDS

If I asked you to list the things dogs need, what would you say; food, shelter, water? These are certainly necessary, but they make up only a fragment of what a dog needs in order to be confident and happy. As a foster, you must provide much more than love and these basic necessities.

Nutrition

Poor nutrition can cause a dog to have physical and behavioral issues. Unfortunately, there is no "one size fits all" dog food. A poor diet can result in a multitude of physical ailments, some of which mimic illnesses entirely unrelated to a nutrition deficit or allergy. These concerning symptoms will have you running to your veterinarian, giving your dog unnecessary medicine and subsequently, paying for unneeded office visits, when the remedy is feeding your dog a more nutritionally balanced meal.

When a dog is not feeling well his symptoms will manifest into poor or lackadaisical behavior. It is difficult to train a dog that is physically ill. Poor ingredients such as low quality meat, too much grain and fillers can be the cause of a behavioral change. When I work with dogs that suffer from aggression or hyperactivity, I first check the ingredients in their food. If it contains too much or low quality protein, sugar, fillers or grain, I generally recommend a diet change. Too much protein can inhibit serotonin from forming, resulting in hyperactivity. Sugar, or beet pulp, can cause hyperactivity and ear infections. These are just a few behavioral problems that I have encountered, and resolved with just a change of food. As always, check with a veterinarian to determine the best solution and correct diagnosis.

I personally feed a natural, raw diet. My dogs get a mixture of human-grade meat and a variety of mixed pulverized vegetables and fruit. I add supplements as needed. This type of diet is not for everyone, because it requires extra time and money. There are many websites and books that can assist you with making your own dog food whether cooked or raw.

If kibble seems to be a better solution to your dog's needs, I recommend a grain-free food that has about 24% protein. The ingredients should list meat first. Be sure you recognize the majority of the ingredients as food and not chemicals.

Always allow thirty days for a dog to transition to a new food. During that transition period, mix the new food with the old and gradually wean him off of the old food. During the first couple of weeks, your dog will go through a "detox" period. During that time, he may have loose stool, an upset stomach, or excessive gas. It is not unusual for a dog to eat the new food heartily for the first couple of days and then back off for a couple of days.

To assist with choosing the best food for your dog, I recommend checking out www.dogfoodanalysis.com.

Expectations

Whether at work or in our personal lives, we, humans want to know what is expected of us. Unsure expectations, equates to the inability to set goals, the loss of confidence and poor decision-making. Dogs must also know what is expected of them, otherwise, they will fill that expectation with behavior they perceive as correct. Or, they will act out in ways that self-reward, as opposed to being rewarded by a human. Humans then perceive the dog as being bad, incorrigible, or untrainable. When dogs fail, humans tend to get upset and cause more stress to the dog. Setting expectations, for both you and the dog, is mandatory for teaching appropriate manners for the real world.

Leadership

Dogs are social and pack animals. In every pack, there is a leader and there are followers. The humans in your home should share the leadership role. The dogs in your home should share the follower's role. Problems arise when you do not assume a confident and consistent leadership position. Every dog in your household should understand that you are in charge of who comes into the pack as well as the safety of the pack.

So, what does it mean to be a leader? Being a leader does not mean you are the "dominant" or "alpha" in the pack. It does not mean you have to prove your position by yelling or by using harsh techniques. As a leader, you do not do alpha rollovers, muzzle grabs, growl or yell. You do not use an "abrasive" tone of voice or tower over your dog. When you raise your voice or put fear into your dog to show leadership, you are proving that you lack the confidence to do it in a calm, confident manner.

Being a leader means you are a consistent, confident individual and you have follow through.

Think about someone you know who is a good leader. Do they put fear into you to get you to follow? Real leaders lead confidently and calmly. They allow their followers to learn to trust them. Leading dogs is quite similar to any other leadership role. You will establish your leadership role through your everyday routine, and develop good habits so your confidence and consistency improve. By controlling the things your dog sees as a reward, and by following through with consequences, you will be predictable so your dogs will see what is expected of him.

Dogs that have a dominant temperament and are natural leaders do not have to be forceful to get respect from other dogs. When I watch my dominant dog, it amazes me how effortlessly she establishes the lead role in a pack. The dogs that surround her automatically know she is in charge. She does this without having to use force and without being a bully.

Follow Through and Consistency

Consistency and follow through are crucial when training. It is important to set expectations that fit into your life, and stick with them. You should have this consistency throughout the day, not just when putting a leash on, or when waiting at the door. This is one of the most difficult lessons I teach. It is not surprising that humans have a hard time with it. Our culture is one of instant gratification and convenience, however, in order to be successful when teaching a dog, you must put in the time and effort. There is no quick fix.

I was making a return visit to a client who was eager to show me how well she had been doing with her two Goldendoodles. I approached the front door and knocked. I heard the dogs barking, and then I heard her tell them to go to their respective beds. When she opened the door to invite me in they both moved from their beds ready to bound to the door. My client calmly closed the door and placed them back onto their beds. Once again, she opened the door. One dog moved from his bed, so she closed the door again. When she opened the door the third time, the dogs, again got up, as I took a step into the house. Instead of closing the door, as she had done the previous two times, she used her body to move them away. She only insisted that they back away from the door and not return to their beds. Within a few seconds I was allowed in the door and was greeted nicely by both.

Her technique was perfect--until the third try. She failed at the follow through by not requiring them to return to their beds. The dogs now think that in order to get a reward (the guest), they must sit by the door, rather than on their beds, since each time they were on their beds the guest did not come in. When I asked her why there was inconsistency in her follow through, she stated that she wanted the dogs to not greet her guest until given permission. She simply wanted them away from the door. All she had to do was decide where she wanted her dogs at the time of her guest's arrival. Were the dogs to be in their beds, or were they to be sitting just inside the door? Once she decided where that spot was, she should follow through, regardless of how many times she would have to shut the door and wait for compliance. Later, I will discuss what to do if a dog continually refuses to respond to your expectations.

Many people will not stick with a specific training technique if it does not work fast enough. When they switch techniques they do not give the dog an opportunity to problem-solve and eliminate the behavior the owner wants extinguished. If you acknowledge a behavior 1 out of 10 times you are sure to see that behavior again. If you ignore that behavior consistently or interrupt appropriately, the behavior will extinguish. Not every behavior will extinguish quickly so be patient with your techniques and give them a chance to work. Be confident and consistent and follow through with the technique until you get the desired result.

Socialization

Dogs are natural pack animals and therefore thrive in environments that support this process. They instinctively know how to communicate properly in order to keep peace and harmony. Like humans, they use communication skills to avoid conflict and solve problems. However, in order to hone these skills they must receive proper socialization with other dogs. Human interaction is extremely important, however, humans cannot replace the essential skills dogs learn from one another. This socialization should include dogs of different ages, sizes, breeds and personalities. Socializing with dogs in the same household is not enough. I recommend regular trips to an experienced daycare, dog park or to dog socials with friends.

Stability

In order for a pack to succeed it must have stability. Leadership and rules must remain consistent, which is why it is important to find healthy, forever homes for foster dogs.

Having stability helps dogs deal with change, unfamiliar situations and other conflicts. You must learn to be stable with your leadership skills and the expectations you set for your foster dog. Before a dog goes into a foster home, your organization should first look at the prospective fosters with a clear and definitive approach. The organization must know the limitations and abilities of each foster home registered in your organization. Pulling dogs that have issues without fosters that can handle them is an organizational faux pas made regularly. Many dogs that come into rescue have behavior issues. The most common I see are fear and anxiety issues. These dogs are desperate for someone to build their confidence and help them to overcome the issues that plague them. When they are in a fear stage they are going to be difficult to adopt. These dogs must have a foster home that provides stability, proper care and training before being ready for adoption.

Mental Stimulation

Many people feel that in order to curb a dog's hyperactivity, they must exercise the dog incessantly. Physical stimulation is important, however, a dog needs mental stimulation as well. In fact, too much physical activity causes a cyclical issue—as the dog's stamina increases, they continue to need more exercise. Dogs' brains are designed to problem-solve, but in today's society we often do not allow our dogs to think for themselves. Trainers who only teach command-based training make dogs robotic in nature. Following a command does not necessarily mean a dog is well mannered, socialized, confident and free of behavioral issues. Properly allowing a dog to think for itself helps produce a dog with the before mentioned attributes.

It is important that we allow dogs to learn and grow by using techniques that are not harsh or scary to them. To help you understand the importance of mental stimulation and how it differs from commanding your dog on a regular basis or punishing him for making the wrong choice, let's look at a puzzle for a human. Let's say that I sit down with you and give you a 500-piece jigsaw puzzle. Each time you get the incorrect puzzle piece I say nothing. The consequence of choosing the wrong piece is that it does not fit. Each time you get the correct puzzle piece I pat you on the back and give you a dollar. At the end of that puzzle, you will not only have $500, but you will also be mentally exhausted. Your skills of putting a puzzle together have improved, you have more confidence with the task, and you have increased your self-control, or focus. The next time you sit down to do a puzzle you will be faster, more confident and you will get less frustrated when you choose the wrong puzzle pieces.

Now let's say that I give you a different jigsaw puzzle with the same number of pieces, but instead of rewarding each correct piece with a dollar I periodically give you a reward.

That dollar is enough of a reward to keep you working the puzzle, much like playing a slot machine. However, instead of ignoring the wrong puzzle piece, I scream and yell at you. How would you feel? Would the reward you receive for the right piece be enough to keep you focused and eager to finish the puzzle? Would you start to feel anxious each time you picked up a piece? Possibly you would choose to walk away and not finish the game. What if I forced you to play the game? Would your confidence drop? Would anxiety increase?

Lastly, let's say, instead of allowing you to choose which piece you want to try, I give you the correct piece and allow you to put it in the correct spot. We accomplish that puzzle together, but what skills have you learned? What will happen when I send you off to do another puzzle by yourself? Would you be successful? How often do you think you would get the wrong piece compared to the right piece? You would have a difficult time, unless I was there leading and guiding you through the entire process.

How does this relate to dogs? Life is a puzzle to a dog. Each time they are faced with a decision, (i.e. how do I get my owner's attention) they must choose a "puzzle piece." Many times this puzzle piece is wrong, but sometimes it is right. When we punish the dog for the wrong puzzle piece, we make them afraid to keep trying. To them, they do not know right and wrong, good or bad; only what works and what does not work. If we constantly tell a dog which puzzle piece to use, such as a command, then we do not allow them to build the skills they need to deal with situations that will arise during their lifetime; situations for which you cannot train.

Problem-Solving Skills:

Dogs that are good problem-solvers learn behaviors more quickly and are more apt to try new things. Dogs that are not good problem-solvers, because they were never given the opportunity, or because they were punished for "putting the wrong piece in the puzzle" will not learn as quickly as a self, confident dog and will cringe at the opportunity to learn new things.

Physical Stimulation:

Every dog needs exercise, but not to keep them calm and well-behaved. Exercise keeps them physically healthy. There is some physical exercise a dog can receive that will require some mental stimulation, such as playing with other dogs, playing fetch with the owner, or a multi-tasking activity such as fly ball or agility. The amount of exercise a dog should receive depends on the individual dog. Some breeds require more exercise while others are satisfied with a calm walk around the neighborhood. Whatever you think your dog needs attempt to meet it on a regular basis however, do not stress if you are unable to give him the same amount every day; the mental stimulation that you are giving him will make up for it.

Self-Control:

Having a dog that listens and responds to your commands is good, but a dog must learn to control himself during moments of arousal, on his own. He cannot wait for you to tell him to "calm down." Self-control plays into everything a dog does. He must have self-control when riding in a car, interacting with other dogs, passing people and other animals while on walks, greeting visitors at the door, and, frankly, anything that requires him to maintain control when physically and mentally aroused. If your dog does not have self-control then he will not be able to respond to commands when in a high arousal state and a distraction prone environment.

CHAPTER 4
DOG COMMUNICATION AND LANGUAGE

Dog Language is the utilization of specific body postures, noises and actions that help a dog to communicate effectively with other dogs and people. A dog's sole purpose for using dog language is to avoid conflict. Dogs perceive conflict differently than humans. Dog conflict may be perceived when another dog or human plays too rough, when a human, animal or object approaches too quickly, or when a human is loud or overly confrontational. Conflict can also be caused by elements in the environment such as thunder, fireworks, cameras or cars. Avoiding conflict does not always mean a dog is trying to thwart a fight, it means he is trying to pacify what makes him uncomfortable. Dogs need to learn how to appropriately communicate with other dogs and conversely, humans need to know how to read this language.

Calming Signals

There are **three levels of calming signals dogs use in order to communicate**. These levels range from passive (Level 1) to aggressive (Level 3). Dog language can be difficult to detect and decipher until you are introduced to it. After which, it becomes obvious and even entertaining.

Dogs offer a *behavior* when they want something, like a treat, a toy, or play. They offer a *signal* when they want to solicit a calming effect.

Level 1 – Passive Signals

Level 1 is the most innate level of signals used, *only if* the dog has had a chance to practice dog language. Many dogs lack proficient communication skills because they do not get adequate interaction with other dogs. Although born with the ability to communicate, dogs must practice these skills on a regular basis. If not, they lack the confidence to control a situation that may escalate into conflict. Dogs with insufficient language skills usually skip Level 1 signals.

Head Turn:

This is the most commonly used signal. A dog will slowly turn his head from side to side, avoiding eye contact. He may do this for many seconds before attempting another signal in order to give the conflict a chance to appropriately diminish. As rescuers, you probably see this signal often when trying to photograph a dog because many dogs see cameras as a conflict. Use this signal to calm a dog that is nervous, shy or overly excited.

Body Turn:

A dog will turn his entire body from a frontal position and show you his side or he may turn all the way around and show you his rear. This is another great signal that you can use to help calm down a dog. This is the most effective technique when dealing with a jumping dog.

Eye Aversion:

This is when a dog will avert his eyes away from you without necessarily turning his head or body. You will often see dogs do this when you have a dog's face in your hands, and he cannot turn his head.

Sit:

Dogs will sit when dealing with a new dog, an overly excited dog or a human who is being too forceful. Many times a sit will become a default behavior when a dog does not know what else to do to appease a situation. To understand if the action is a signal or a behavior, look at the rest of the body. If it is used as a signal, the dog will use it with another signal like turning the head or averting the eyes. If it is a behavior, the dog will sit and look towards the other dog or human. This is a great signal to use when dealing with nervous or shy dogs. Instead of sitting, I recommend squatting so it is easier to move away or closer to the dog depending on the response he is giving you. When you squat, you will always use another signal like head turning, body turning or averting the eyes.

Down:

This signal is not as common as the previous. Little dogs are more likely to use the down as a signal or behavior than a larger dog. Dogs with a high level of confidence will also be more likely to use this signal. Like a sit, you will see other behaviors combined with it. Always look at the rest of the body and in what context the down is being used.

Bow:

This can be used as a signal or as a behavior. When used as a signal, a dog will go into the bow position where his front legs are stretched out in front and his bottom is up in the air. However, unlike a play bow where a dog will jump from side-to-side quickly as a play invitation, a dog will remain stationary when using a bow as a calming signal. When it is a signal, you will often times see it mixed with another signal like averting eyes or turning the head. Dogs that have very good dog skills will sometimes use a bow as a signal and behavior at the same time. He may want another dog to play, but if the other dog is anxious, the bowing dog may offer a calming signal to relieve the tension of the encounter. You can use this as a signal yourself, but you may feel silly doing it. I recommend using the more natural signals like head and body turns, eye aversion and sitting/squatting.

Quick Licks:

This signal is difficult to see until you are used to spotting it. A quick lick is when the tongue comes out of the mouth and in a very quick motion licks the nose and then quickly moves back in. A dog that uses this will do it several times in a row to try and get his point across. Quick licks will also be combined with other signals.

Raised Paw:

This signal is not used as often as the others. When a dog is using this as a signal, he will slightly raise the paw and use another signal with it. Keep in mind you must read the entire body in order to identify this as a calming signal. If the dog is a pointer, for instance, a raised paw may mean the dog is simply pointing something.

Doing Something Else (Ignoring):

A dog will do this when he wants to extinguish a behavior. He may sniff the ground, urinate and/or completely ignore what it is he wants to extinguish. Many people see this as a dog being stubborn but in most cases, the dog is trying to calm a situation. For example, your dog, Jake, is playing in the yard and you call him to you. He does not listen to you the first three times. Why? He may not know the command. Or, if he does, you could be using a harsh tone that he views as a conflict. If the latter is correct, Jake will ignore you and wait for you to calm down.

Yawning:

Dogs yawn for two reasons. He may yawn because he is tired or as a signal to calm a situation or himself. Look at what context the yawn is being used to help you decide if it is a signal or a behavior. On occasion, a dog will use this with other signals.

Curving:

When meeting a new dog or sometimes, a new person, a dog will curve towards the object to show calmness and friendliness. This is where dogs will greet one another by smelling their rear ends or genitalia. This seems rude to us, but in reality, meeting face-to-face is inappropriate and confrontational in a dog's world. Many dogs, especially puppies, are not good at this signal due to a lack of experience and maturity. Poor greeting signals will often start a scuffle. Use this method when meeting a new dog. Walking up to the dog from the side, and curving to greet him. Do not approach a strange dog from the front. And I suggest that you never bend over a dog that you are unfamiliar with its temperament.

Splitting Up:

If you have ever had a dog sit or stand between you and another person, (i.e. while cuddling on the couch with your significant other), you have probably seen this signal. Many people think this is a cute gesture of jealousy, however the dog actually sees this as a conflict and is trying to *literally* split you apart. During play, dogs will do this when they sense other dogs' rough play will cause a fight. Confident, experienced dogs will walk between two dogs, and will stay with the offending dog until it redirects, much like an umpire during a sporting match. This signal takes a lot of practice as most dogs lack the consistency, confidence and follow-through to do it properly. The more a dog has a chance to interact with other dogs, the better he will become.

Level 2 - Less Passive Signals

Level 2 signals are less passive and very easily recognized. Many humans become uncomfortable when they see Level 2 signals, often labeling a dog as vicious. Dogs will use Level 2 signals if they do not, 1. Have confidence, 2. The time to use Level 1 signals, or 3. To articulate to the other dog that his patience is growing thin.

Growling:

A dog will give a low growl to let another dog or person know he is uncomfortable. This means that the dog is *trying* to control a potentially conflicting situation. When growling is used as a signal it is mixed with other signals such as a head turn. If growling is a behavior, other signals are not used, and the dog's posture will be stiff and he will stare at the person or dog ahead of him. If you have a patient dog with good dog language, he will often try Level 1 signals first. If using Level 1 signals is not effective, he will be forced to escalate to Level 2. For example, if a family pet is constantly harassed by a child at home, (say the child is crawling all over him, chasing him down, getting in his face, etc.), and the dog's Level 1 signals are being ignored, the dog will be forced to escalate to Level 2. When the dog growls at the child, the family scolds the dog instead of educating the child, or they improperly assume the dog is vicious, and re-home the dog or worse. This scenario is one that occurs all too often. It is important to know whether the dog had previously displayed Level 1 signals prior to the growl, and before jumping to Level 2.

Snarling:

A snarl occurs when a dog pulls his lips up and shows his teeth. This signal is often used with a low growl and always with a Level 1 signal such as a quick lick, head turn or eye aversion. Many fearful dogs with no confidence will resort to this behavior immediately when faced with an uncomfortable situation. Dogs with confidence will use a snarl if they do not have time to use a Level 1 signal, (i.e. when another dog is suddenly in his face). Like the growl, if it is not mixed with other signals, it is being given as a behavior with the possibility of turning into aggression.

Level 3 – Aggressive Signals

Level 3 is considered the Aggressive Level. When a dog uses Level 3 signals, it does not mean he is vicious, it just means that the signals are much more noticeable to the untrained eye. Dogs use this Level when Levels 1 and 2 did not work or he does not have the patience or skills to do Levels 1 and 2 first. Level 3 signals are very obvious and often make people nervous. Because of their lack of understanding, they will often punish or correct a dog for offering Level 3 signals. This will normally make the dog resort to level 3 faster than usual, because of the association of correction or punishment when another dog gets too close. Level 3 signals can also be behaviors from a dog that is being a bully so you must read the dog's entire body to understand.

Muzzle Grab:

A muzzle grab occurs when a dog attempts to place his mouth over another dog's muzzle. This may be a sign of dominance because it places another dog into a submissive position. Humans sometimes use a version of this by purchasing head halters that go over the muzzle of their dog. This is placed into the aggressive level, because there is physical contact between the dogs. Though the dog giving signals does not intend to cause harm, the dog receiving the muzzle grab will oftentimes get a cut on the bridge of the muzzle because the skin is thin in this area. This behavior is acceptable when the previous two levels have not worked. Most young puppies experience this at least once in their life. If you observe a dog is not respecting Level 1 and 2 signals, you should correct the disrespectful dog—not the dog giving the signals.

Snapping:

When giving this signal a dog will snap towards whatever needs calming, and then back away quickly. This occurs when humans who do not understand that the dog has been displaying Level 1 and 2 signals and continue to place the dog in an uncomfortable and stressful environment. When the conflict is not resolved, then the dog will escalate to snapping. A dog at this level is usually snapping out of fear, or lacks the confidence and maturity to disengage emotionally from what is causing the fear. Essentially, all he wants is to avoid conflict and to make something go away. The dog that uses snapping as a behavior, will often not back down after snapping. This is the difference between a dog using proper dog language or getting caught up in his fear turning dangerously aggressive. This is also the number one signal that is used when a dog has no confidence or does not understand the first two levels.

Biting:

Often times biting is a dog's last resort when other signals have not worked. Like a dog that uses a snap, dogs with low confidence or language skills often bite instead of offering Level 1 or 2 signals. If a dog is using this as a signal, the dog will often bite and then back off. I define a bite as a snap with contact. A signal bite is different than a warning bite. A dog that is using the bite as a warning behavior will hold and shake its victim and not back down. A hold and shake will cause more damage than a signal bite and release.

When observing any Level 3 signals, you must not jump to conclusions. Level 3 signals do not necessarily mean that the dog is vicious and cannot be rehabilitated. You must evaluate the dog carefully to adequately evaluate why the dog used this level of signals or behavior. Is he offering Level 1 and 2 first or is he going immediately to Level three? The more you observe, the more competent you will be at evaluating the dog.

Non-Calming Signals

Dogs give other dogs and humans various signals that help them communicate. These signals are not necessarily calming signals, and are typically easy to recognize.

Tail Wag:

This is the most misunderstood signal. A tail wag does not always mean "happy dog". A tail wag means a dog is aroused in one form or another. When evaluating what a particular tail wag means look at the entire body for confirmation. Also, take a dog's breed into consideration. Many dogs do not have tails, and others normally have a stiff or curled tail.

If a dog's tail is **slow and relaxed**, the dog is comfortable in the current situation. I also refer to this as the "flag" wag, because it often looks like a flag blowing in the wind.

A **high, stiff and slow wag** means the dog is being

challenging or taking a defensive posture. If it is not moving, the dog could be trying to calm another dog. I refer to this wag as a "stick in low wind."

A **high, stiff and fast wag** means a dog is highly aroused. Arousal can come from a variety of sources. This is also known as the "stick in a hurricane" wag.

A **Fast to moderate and relaxed** wags means a dog is happy and comfortable. Often times the wag will make a circle, which is why I refer to this as a "circle wag."

If a dog has a **low/no wag,** the dog is uncomfortable from fear or nervousness. A low/no wag can also come from pain. Sometimes the tail will be tucked between the legs.

Raised Hackles:
At some point you will see the fur on the back or neck of a dog stand up. This is a natural response to arousal. Arousal can be from excitement, being unsure, low confidence, and/or aggression. A dog that has his hackles raised is not necessarily getting ready to attack. You must always read the entire body of a dog to really understand what he is trying to communicate. Again, you must be aware of the breed. Breeds such as Rhodesian ridgebacks have raised fur all the time.

Shake Off:

Shake offs are used as a "release" which can denote the beginning of play or the end of a sequence of events, (i.e. after a long introduction, a dog shakes off to show he is ready for play).

Barking:

Dog use barking as a vocal way to communicate. Keep in mind a mastiff and a Chihuahua will have different low-pitched barks:

A **high-pitched bark** indicates excitement, heavy arousal, fearfulness or nervousness.

A **low-pitched bark** is used for warning or frustration.

Distance Increasing Signals

These signals are used to increase the distance between a dog and a conflict. When a dog is uncomfortable with something (i.e. another dog that is too close), he will use these signals as a way to express his desire to be away from the conflict.

Whining, Yelping and Crying:

These will often come from insecure puppies or dogs that are unable to use calming signals properly. Crying and whining is a vocal way of demonstrating frustration and not used for distance increasing. Yelping can be associated with pain, (think about the last time you accidentally stepped on your dog's tail).

Humans Can Speak Dog!

Humans are capable of communicating with dogs by using these same signals. Whether you have a dog that is afraid, nervous or outgoing, you can calm him by using these same signals. Practice using these signals with your own dog until they become second nature to you. Start by seeing how well your dog responds to them. How well they respond will tell you how well they know dog language, as well as help you improve your own skills. Use only Level 1 signals with your dog and be sure to be confident and consistent!

A **head turn** is easy to use with a jumping or nervous dog. Be sure to completely ignore the dog (no touching or talking) while using this signal.

A **body turn** is a great way to deal with a jumping dog. When the dog sits for 3-5 seconds, verbally acknowledge the dog for being good. If the dog jumps again, turn your body and ignore him. If the dog is causing you pain from jumping, ignore the dog and walk to another room.

Use a **sit or squat** with a nervous or fearful dog (if they are not oversized.) Always keep your body turned to the side.

In order for **yawning** to work, you must be consistent. Mix this with another signal such as a head turn. You can use this signal to your advantage when dealing with a nervous or shy dog. For instance, if a dog is afraid of thunderstorms, make sure the dog is near you. Simply ignore the dog (do not coddle), and yawn from time to time. You may see the dog begin to yawn back. He is trying to calm himself.

Again, **curving** should always be used when meeting a new dog. Approach the dog from the side, and curve to greet. Do not approach a dog head on.

Split ups should not be overused. It is essential that you are confident and consistent when walking in between two dogs. Follow-though is crucial in order for this signal to work. For example, if your dog is barking at a door, confidently position yourself between the dog and the door. Move your body toward the dog until it redirects. Do not talk or touch the dog. If the dog gets around you and returns to the door, do not panic. Simply start over.

CHAPTER 5
SETTING EXPECTATIONS

Before you begin training, you should first decide what you expect from a dog. Focus on what behaviors you want to see rather than the ones you do not. Setting a dog's expectations starts with knowing what those expectations are going to be. Make a list of desirable behaviors so the entire household knows what is considered acceptable.

For instance, how do you want your dog to act...

1. ...when someone comes to the door?
2. ... when you are eating dinner?
3. ...when you bring a new dog into your home?

Your answers will vary based on what you feel will ensure the dog will get adopted. Below are some sample answers to these questions:

1. Barking is a natural form of communication for dogs. I never mind a dog letting me know when someone is outside or at my door, but I do expect him to have some control. Once I acknowledge what the dog is alerting me to I want him to quiet down.

If this was your stated expectation for barking, then you

are well on your way to achieving the goal! Keep in mind; do not list the behaviors you *do not* want the dog to do. Instead list the behavior you *do want* your dog to do.

2. During dinner, I want to see my dog lying down with his head on the floor.

Perhaps you do not mind if your dog is staring at you as long as his head is on the floor. Or, perhaps you prefer your dog to be on his bed. These are the things you need to think about prior to any training, so that you and the household are on the same page prior to and during training.

3. I expect my dog to behave in an accepting fashion when
I bring a new dog into my home whether it be a foster or a friend's dog. The territory belongs to me and I want my dog to accommodate another dog without being territorial, insecure and aggressive.

Again, you are stating what is expected of the dog and then what behavior will be trained. You will accomplish this goal by helping the dogs in your home practice dog language and by being a confident leader.

Your list of expectations may differ from this list. That is okay. Just be consistent and focus on what you want as the end result.

CHAPTER 6
BASICS OF TRAINING

When most people train their dog they focus on the basics of sit, stay, down, come and heel. These behaviors are beneficial, but they do not necessarily set the dog up for success in the real world. Because a dog will sit on command in a kitchen at dinnertime does not mean he will have self-control and sit when guests arrive, let alone if they bring a strange dog. This is why it is imperative that you build a foundation that allows the dog to extrapolate proper behaviors in all areas of his life.

Secrets to the REWARD

Dog trainers and behavioral consultants often debate what the proper reward for a dog is that offers a desired behavior. Traditional trainers scoff at the thought of using food or treats, because they consider it bribery. However, they often misunderstand the proper way to use it. Any reward can be used as bribery or as a lure. The real answer is; it does not matter what you use for a reward as long as your dog finds it desirable. Your job is to reward properly.

I teach three ways to acknowledge good behavior: 1. A verbal mark, such as "good boy/girl." 2. A verbal mark with petting. 3. A verbal mark with a resource, such as food or a toy.

Rewarding properly will help your dog understand what behaviors you want to see repeated. When you get into the habit of telling him "yes" or "good" for proper behavior, he will focus and repeat that behavior in hopes of receiving your attention (a reward). Think of yourself as a slot machine--pay out intermittently, but pay out big. For instance, your dog performs a proper behavior ten times. Of those ten behaviors, you reward him four times with food, three times with a pet, and three times with a positive verbal mark. This is variable reinforcement, or what I like to call, "the slot machine system." The dog anticipates a reward, but does not know which reward will be divvied out. This heightens his desire to do as he is instructed.

Never have food in your hand when waiting for your dog to offer a behavior. You may have it on a counter, in a bowl or put away in a cabinet, but focus on marking the good behavior first before worrying about what type of food reward you are going to give.

All dogs are motivated by food. If your dog is not eating his regular food, it does not mean he is not food motivated, it means he either does not like the taste of his food or it is causing him discomfort. I recommend trying a variety of healthy, and nutritional foods to see what works best. A food reward should be a treat small enough to be consumed quickly and yet large enough to taste. "Jackpot" rewards (consisting of a handful of small treats and dispensed with an overabundance of enthusiasm) can be used, but sparingly. A jackpot will leave a big impression on the dog and will raise the likelihood that the behavior will be repeated.

I recommend putting together a mix of different treats I call a "doggie Chex Mix." These treats should vary in flavors and textures.

Secrets to using CONSEQUENCES

Training consists of positive and negative responses. People typically associate positive with "good" and negative with "bad." Think of positive and negative in mathematical terms instead. Positive means "to add" and negative means "to take away." Giving a positive response or consequence means you give the dog something it wants, (i.e. attention or a treat.) Negative responses or consequences occur when you take something away. For instance, by ignoring you are taking attention away. People often think negative consequences only consist of harsh punishment such as the use of a correction collar, a knee in the chest or a zap from an electronic collar. These are negative in a traditional sense ("bad"), and typically do not facilitate the learning process. By using harsh methods, you are only teaching the dog to avoid pain by suppressing certain behaviors. Often dogs will shut down or stop trying to problem solve because of fear. These definitions will make it easier to understand the difference in positive and negative consequences:

Positive Reinforcement:

When using this technique you are adding something good to the dog to get a behavior repeated. For example, when your dog sits and you give him a treat or praise.

Negative Reinforcement:

When using negative reinforcement you are taking away something unpleasant in order to get the dog to repeat a behavior. For instance, shocking a dog with an e-collar until it comes, or chocking a dog with a collar until he sits. I never recommend these methods because they are dangerous and out of date.

Positive Punishment:

Positive punishment occurs when you add something unpleasant to extinguish a behavior. When traditional trainers use leash pops to extinguish pulling on leash or a zap by an e-collar to extinguish barking, they are using positive punishment. I do not recommend this type of punishment because, like negative reinforcement, it can also extinguish a dog's desire to try new behaviors because it causes fear. I also do not use positive punishment because in order for it to be successful a person must know how to use proper timing and how not to harm a dog physically.

Negative Punishment:

By taking away something good from the dog in order to extinguish a behavior you are using negative punishment. You can show a dog that is jumping on you that the behavior is not acceptable by utilizing a body turn and ignoring. By doing this you are taking away something good—attention.

When training, you should use positive reinforcement and negative punishment only. This will allow you to be less than perfect with your timing and still receive results. Always remain calm, confident and consistent when giving consequences.

There are a number of consequences you can use when you see a behavior from your dog that you wish to extinguish. Keep in mind that not every dog is going to see something as a consequence, so you have to do a little problem-solving yourself to determine the best one to use. For instance, taking attention away from a dog that does not seem to crave attention will not help extinguish a behavior, however, taking away a treat may. Here are some consequences you can use to extinguish an undesirable behavior:

- Taking attention away from the dog
- Putting dog in time-out
- Not putting on leash
- Not taking off leash
- Not throwing toy
- Not feeding
- Not allowing out of crate
- Stopping play

As I mentioned above, ignoring (not looking or touching the dog) is a technique to use to extinguish behavior that is not self-rewarding, (a behavior such as chewing is self-rewarding) but you must do it correctly.

Self-rewarding behavior is a behavior the dog does that rewards without you being involved. When dealing with self-rewarding behaviors, such as chewing or barking, you cannot simply ignore the dog. You must interrupt these behaviors instead of ignoring them. Even when you interrupt you do not have to do it harshly. Interrupt with the least amount of interaction so that the dog does not interpret your acknowledgement as a reward.

A common self-rewarding behavior is counter surfing

when food is present. If there is nothing on the counter, within the dog's reach, the behavior is not self-rewarding. There is nothing to gain. If this is the case, ignore the behavior. The dog will learn that nothing is on the counter and will eventually stop trying. For those times when the dog is successful at getting food off of the counter, you can either push the item farther back or you can implement a split-up between the dog and the counter, interrupting his attempt. You do not want to talk to the dog during this exercise because you need to interrupt with the least amount of interaction. You want the dog to learn that counter surfing never works, not that it works unless someone is there to interrupt.

If your dog is chewing on the rug, give a calm "nope," gently remove the dog from the object being chewed on, and give him something else to chew on. Expect the dog to go back to the rug as he tries to figure out why you interrupted him. When he does, simply interrupt again. When the dog does it three times in a row implement a time-out.

Puppies often chew in order to soothe the pain of teething. I recommend having a variety of toys on hand. For older dogs, supply deer antlers or hard bones.

By teaching these real life manners a dog is more likely to stay in his forever home.

Implementing a TIME-OUT

A time-out occurs when a dog is isolated from an event for a certain amount of time due to an inappropriate behavior. Time-outs can be used anywhere for anything. There are rules that you must follow, in order to make it successful.

I use a "three strikes and you are out" rule. Once I give a dog three chances to do the correct behavior by ignoring or interrupting, I implement a time-out. Most time-outs are done for self-rewarding behaviors.

When giving a time-out, be sure you do not show emotion. A true leader does not show emotion when giving a negative consequence. Remain calm and matter-of-fact. Use either a leash, the collar, or if the dog is small enough, carry him to his time-out space; be sure you do not pet or talk to him in the process. If you use the collar, grab the side and use the slightest pressure possible. Do not grab the dog by the scruff.

Time-out areas can change depending on your circumstances. When at home, use a crate or small room as the isolation space. The dog will not see the crate or room as a negative unless you display anger or frustration. If you are out in public you can use your car, a portable crate or just take the dog away from the action and have him stand beside you on leash. If you are at the dog park and the dog misbehaves three times, put him on leash and take him outside the dog park.

When giving time-outs, start with thirty-second intervals and increase as needed. When a time-out is completed, ensure the dog earns his freedom by exhibiting self-control, and that he receives a permission word such as "okay." Do not be surprised if your dog attempts the inappropriate behavior again; he is only trying to figure out what caused the time-out. Once you have given your dog several opportunities with the "three strikes rule" and the dog begins to understand what behaviors are inappropriate, commence with decreasing to two strikes, then one strike and eventually immediate time-out. Most dogs do not get to the immediate time-out when the technique is used properly.

A time-out is appropriate when you are teaching your dog to stop jumping on the furniture. When the dog jumps on the furniture, remove him without speaking. Once he is on the floor, go back about your business. If he continues to jump on the furniture, remove him two more times. When he gets on the furniture a fourth time, take him to his crate or to an isolated room. Leave him for thirty seconds. If he is calm, release him with a permission word, and repeat if necessary. Allow three strikes for the first few days, and then decrease the chances until he begins to understand what you want.

If you are out in public you may have to be more creative. Let's say you ask the dog to sit. If your dog understands the command and refuses, give him three chances and then implement a time-out. If your car is close by, put him in it. If you have a crate, use that. Whatever you do, be sure you do not allow anything good to take place until he sits on his own without you forcing him. Once he is released, take him back to the exact place you asked for the sit and ask for it again. Repeat the process until he does it on his own on the first request.

Remember, time-outs are a useful tool. Do them with confidence and always follow through. Whoever puts the dog in time-out gets the dog out of time-out. If you feel totally exasperated, leave the dog in its time out longer. I would rather you keep the dog in the crate for a longer period of time than scream, yell or give in to an inappropriate behavior.

CHAPTER 7
USE OF TRAINING TOOLS

There is an assortment of training tools on the market that serve a variety of purposes. Use tools that assist in the ease of training your dog. However, be attentive to tools that cause undue pain, and impede your training. Select tools that are particular to the dog you are training and the issues he may have. There is no "one size fits all" training tool. I do recommend that you use the least number of tools to reach your goal.

Leash:

Although a leash is a part of a dog's everyday life, used properly, a leash can be an excellent training tool. A short leash limits your dog's options and therefore, a greater chance to make the right decision. A long or retractable leash permits your dog to self-reward, allows him free rein to a multitude of distractions, and hence, an increased chance to make a wrong decision. The essence of positive training is that you create an environment where the dog makes good decisions and is subsequently rewarded for those decisions. For this reason, you have to eliminate extraneous stimuli that will distract your dog. A short leash sets your dog up for success and promotes a rewarding relationship between you and your canine partner.

Start with a short (12 -24 inch) leash, and work towards something longer.

Dogs spend a lot of time on a leash, which makes it difficult to adopt a dog without leash manners. Poor leash manners is a common complaint from most pet owners, so it is likely that your rescue will be lacking in this area.

In order to use a tool like a leash successfully, you should first know what a leash is and is not. A leash is a length of material that connects you to your dog, and limits where he can or cannot go. The leash is NOT a correction tool. You should never correct your dog by "popping" the leash (jerking it upward in a quick motion).

To get your dog to enjoy his leash you must first refine your leash handling techniques.

Most of my clients use a 1'-3' leash. Use the handle of the leash the way it was intended--with your hand. Do not slip the lead over your wrist and do not wrap it around your hand. Hold it loosely and with as few fingers as possible. Practice putting the leash on your dog inside the house, sit on the couch and just get comfortable holding the leash by the handle.

Next, walk with your feet shoulder width apart and with your hand at your side. Let your entire body maintain control of the dog on the leash, not just your arm and hand. If your arm moves away from your body, anchor your thumb in your belt loop or pocket until you get comfortable walking your dog with your arm by your side.

Correction Collar:

    Choke chains and prong collars are the most common tools purchased, even though many people do not know how to use them correctly. When the dog pulls or exhibits a poor behavior the collar tightens around his neck causing discomfort. The collar can be tightened by the dog moving too far ahead or by the owner jerking the leash backwards or upwards. Often, these collars are not fitted or used properly, and are used as a permanent management tool, rather than a temporary training tool. Correction collars are a form of positive punishment. The owner is applying an uncomfortable stimulus in order to stop an unwanted behavior, such as pulling, lunging, barking or not obeying a command. When a correction collar is too large, the collar hits the dog in the throat, which can result in serious injury. Correction collars teach a dog how to avoid the correction and not how to do a particular behavior. Many people claim that their dog will walk perfectly on a leash, as long as a correction collar is used. It is difficult to teach, off-leash manners to a dog that will only walk properly when a correction collar is used.

Head-Collar:

    Head-collars are used to prevent a dog from pulling and

lunging. These collars are similar to a horse halter and will control the dog with no pain and little discomfort. Head collars are great to use if you have a dog that is too strong to teach proper leash behavior. This tool can give you a positive experience quickly, however, once again, many people tend to use it as a management tool, instead of a teaching tool. I encourage you to not use one unless you absolutely have to. If you do, try to transition the dog to a regular collar in a few weeks. I recommend Premier's Gentle Leader, because it fits the dog properly.

Clicker:

The clicker method of training has been around for many years. It is based on operant conditioning, first introduced by B.F. Skinner. Operant conditioning, also known as instrumental conditioning, is a method of learning that is shaped through reward and punishment. Through operant conditioning, an association is made between a behavior and a consequence for that behavior. A consequence can be bad or good.

A clicker is associated with something good that the dog wants, (i.e. a treat). When the dog offers a behavior that we want to see, the clicker is used to mark that behavior, and a treat is dispensed. The dog learns that each time he hears the click, he will earn a yummy reward. In turn, the dog will continue to offer the behavior to see what makes the clicker click. Clickers are used to teach manners, agility, search and rescue, and more.

Clicker training is also used with humans through a process called TAG. This stands for "Teaching with Acoustical Guidance." A teacher will click at the precise moment a correct behavior occurs. The clicking sound becomes an acoustical binary message, a sort of "snapshot" that is quickly processed by the brain. Regardless of age or application, the TAG trained student learns to react accurately with lightning speed while building muscle memory and confidence.

When used with dogs, the clicker method of training solidifies behaviors in a short amount of time. In order to be successful with the clicker you must have excellent timing; marking a good behavior the instance that it happens.

The biggest myth with clicker training is that you always have to have a clicker with you to mark behavior. In reality, you do not. You can use a word as a verbal marker, such as "yes." As with other tools, use the clicker less and less, as the dog learns what each command means and what behaviors are appropriate. I encourage you to try this tool. It is fun and you will see quick results. Below is a quick guide to using the clicker:

1. To teach a dog that the clicker means positive rewards you must first *charge* it by clicking and treating any behavior up to ten times in a row. Do not worry about what behavior you are clicking as long as it is something you would like to see again.
2. Click during a desired behavior, not after it has occurred. Click as the dog is sitting, the paw is being raised for a shake or as the dog is lowering himself to lie down.
3. Click once and reward with a food reward. To show extra enthusiasm you may click once and give a "jackpot."
4. Click for ANY behavior you would like to see repeated, even if you do not know what you want to do with it or what you would name it.
5. Do not punish for behavior that you do not want, just ignore it.
6. Allow the dog to offer behavior on his own, do not give commands during your exercises.
7. Do not click to get your dog's attention.
8. Do not use the clicker to give a command.

E-Collar:

It is my belief that e-collars, also known as electronic collars or shock collars, should never be sold to the general public. When used carelessly or without knowledge, they can shut down a dog and cause more harm than good.

E-collars are used as a form of positive punishment. A stimulus is added to stop a behavior in the form of an electric shock. The concept is to punish the dog when it does not respond to the correct behavior--even if the dog does not understand what he is supposed to be doing. Like many tools, I have seen owners and professionals alike depend too much on the e-collar and never train the dog off of it. When this happens, the dog has been trained to avoid the correction--not to do the correct behavior.

I am opposed to this type of training except as a last resort for a behavior that could be fatal to a dog and subsequently, injurious to a human. In almost two decades of training dogs, I have only used an e-collar twice. If a dog does need an e-collar, a professional who is trained to use the tool should be the one to administer it. To get the desired result, an electric shock should be administered judiciously. Dogs should never wear an e-collar as a usual routine.

No-Pull Harness:

These tools work similar to the head-collar, but fit around the chest rather than the muzzle. Unless a dog has an existing neck or throat injury, I do not typically recommend a harness because they were originally produced to make it easier and more comfortable for dogs to pull sleds. When a dog is wearing a harness they are able to pull with their entire body instead of just their neck. Go with a head-collar if you need a tool to make leash walking easier.

Martingale Collar:

Martingale, or "no-slip" collars, are great tools to use when you have a dog that can easily escape from his regular collar. This collar was originally made for Greyhounds because of the small circumference of their necks. I use this collar often when working with rescues or shelter pets. The collar has no buckle or quick snap, and is fitted by sliding it over the dog's head. It fits right behind the dog's ears and the leash is attached to an o-ring. When the dog pulls, the collar tightens preventing the dog from backing out of it. I use this type of collar because it not only prevents a dog from escaping, but it also does not harm a dog like a choke or pinch collar. I recommend putting a regular buckle or quick-snap collar on a dog when it is not being walked, and only use a Martingale collar for walking and teaching purposes. Do not use this as a correction collar.

CHAPTER 8
REAL LIFE MANNERS

Feeding for Leadership:

As a leader, it is your responsibility to provide food. Feeding on a schedule is a good way to keep an eye on what your dog is consuming as well as letting him know that you are the leader. When I say schedule, I do not mean feed the same time every day. I mean, feed at different times every day, and make each feeding a training session. You want your dog to know that feeding happens when you are ready, not because of what his internal clock says. Feeding at different times in the morning and at different times in the evening.

There are two ways to feed your dog. Regular feeding occurs when you place the bowl on the floor allowing the dog to eat it all, at one time. Hand-feeding occurs when the dog has to work for each bite of food he receives. Hand-feeding is a technique that should be done the very first week with your foster dog. The goal of feeding for leadership is for your dog to learn problem-solving techniques as well as show self-control. This is the foundation of *all* training.

Hand-Feeding:

Hand-feeding addresses leadership, problem-solving and self-control. It gives you a chance to acknowledge behaviors that you would like to see repeated, whether they are tricks or good manners.

The goal of hand feeding is to train your dog to think about his actions and to make good decisions. Do not give any obedience commands. Sit with the food on your lap and wait quietly. Do not have the food in your hand. Keep the bowl in your lap. If your dog moves toward the bowl, simply cover it with your hands.

You want the dog to offer behaviors in order to receive any food. You dog will throw a number of behaviors. He will run in circles, bark, sit, lay down, roll over, and so forth. For the behaviors you want extinguished, simply ignore the dog. For the behaviors that you like, mark them verbally ("good" or "yes") or with a clicker, and then give the dog a small bite of food. If you are feeding soft or homemade food, use a spoon. Timing is essential. Mark *during* the desired behavior, and not after it is completed or as the dog moves onto another behavior. For example, if you like for your dog to sit, wait for him to begin to sit. As the dog's bottom is moving towards the floor, mark it with "yes" and give him a piece of food. Reward all positive behavior. ANY behavior that you do not mind seeing again, no matter how small, need to be marked. Good manners can be walking by the cat without chasing it, or not barking at a noise outside. These are behaviors that you want to see repeated and the new owners would appreciate, so mark and feed.

Lastly, the dog must do something physically different to earn a mark and a piece of food. He is not allowed to just sit and stare at you. This means he is not problem solving, but simply waiting to be fed. If your dog does not want to work for the food, he does not eat. If this happens several times than you need to change his food.

Let's break this exercise down into steps:

1. Grab your dog's food bowl and fill it up with his normal amount of food for that feeding.
2. Sit somewhere comfortable, where your dog is going to have plenty of room to work. You do not have to sit on the floor.
3. Place the bowl in your lap and use your hands to cover the bowl, *if* the dog is trying to put his nose in it. Do not move the bowl out of the dog's reach or tell the dog to leave it. He is offering an inappropriate behavior, so, simply cover the bowl and ignore him.
4. Stay silent throughout the process until your dog gives you a behavior that you would like to see repeated. When he offers a behavior that you want, mark it with your marker and give a piece of food.
5. Wait for him to offer something different and repeat.
6. If he gives you a behavior that you do not like followed by a good behavior, be sure the good behavior is exhibited for at least three seconds before recognizing.

The pause only happens if the good is following a bad behavior.

This process may take between 15-45 minutes, depending on the dog's confidence level and problem-solving skills. When beginning this technique feed the entire bowl this way. Do not feed half the bowl by hand and then place the bowl down for the remainder of the feeding. If your dog does not earn all of his food in the time allotted, put the food away and try again later. It is not unusual for a new dog to leave a portion of his food. I recommend feeding this way, at least once a day, unless you have a very nervous or shy dog, then hand feed both feedings.

Regular Feeding:

Just because you allow a dog to eat all of his food at once does not mean he gets it without working for it. Instead of working for each bite, make sure he shows self-constraint before the bowl is placed on the floor and before you give him permission to eat. Allow him twenty minutes to eat and then pick up the bowl.

The dog should sit or down. The dog must remain in that position until permission is given to eat. Your permission word should be consistent. I use "okay." The dog does not have to stay in this position while he eats.

1. Fill your dog's food bowl.
2. Stand still, holding the bowl firmly in hand, and remain quiet. Do not shake the bowl, do not talk to the dog and do not hold the bowl over your dog's head. Wait until your dog sits or lies down; immediately begin lowering the bowl to the floor. Stay a couple of feet from your dog in case he attempts to move toward the bowl.
3. If your dog comes out of position, pick the bowl up. Again, say nothing.
4. When your dog gets back in the appropriate position, begin lowering the bowl. You may continue lowering the bowl as long as the dog is in position, but the second he comes out of position without permission, pick up the bowl.
5. As soon as you get the bowl to the ground, give your permission word, and allow your dog to eat.
6. Each time you do this, require your dog to wait longer before earning permission. Do not become predictable in the amount of time you make the dog wait before eating.

If your dog has hip issues or finds it difficult to sit, you may do this in the stand position. Do not allow the dog to eat until he is standing in the same place. Each time he moves toward the bowl without permission, pick up the bowl.

If you have multiple dogs, teach the exercise individually and slowly put them together, as a group, requiring them to all wait together.

Allowing Pet In/Out Door, Crate and Car:

As a leader you control all rewards. Dogs perceive going outside or coming inside as a reward. Many times, owners allow their dogs to come and go as they please. They do this with either a dog door, or they allow their dog to go out, or come in without permission. This not only demeans your leadership status, it is dangerous.

If you have to hold your dog's collar or give him a command so that he does not bound out the door, then you are not allowing your dog to problem-solve and think for himself. Dogs should learn that going out a door is not an option, unless he is given permission to do so. You should control any threshold that the dog has to cross.

The first step is to establish a permission word. Again, I use "okay." Food will not be used during this exercise since the reward is the ability to move over a threshold.

Start this exercise on leash so that you can limit your dog's ability to move away from the door. Do not use the leash to control where the dog is standing, or to pull the dog away or through the door. Use a leash that limits the dog's movement to only a foot or two ahead of you. Slip your hand into the handle and tuck your thumb into your pocket. Keep the leash loose so that it looks like a 'J' hanging next to his collar. Do not ask your dog to sit for this exercise; in "real life," your dog will be confronted with many open door opportunities, and in those situations, he will more than likely be standing.

Next, start to open the door. Expect your dog to move forward. The moment he moves forward, close the door. Be quick, but try not to slam his head in the door. When the door begins to close he should back up; if he does not, do not pull him back with the leash. Give him a few seconds to back up by gently pushing the door into him. If that does not make him back up, remove your hand from the door and take a step or two backwards with your thumb still hooked in your pocket. This will make him back up with you. Once he is back inside, close the door. Immediately begin opening the door again. Each time he moves forward close the door until he backs up. You may or may not get the door all the way closed before he starts backing up. The moment he backs up, begin opening it again. Be sure your timing is correct. Open the door when the dog is away from it, and close it if he moves forward. Once the dog is stationary, and you have the door open enough for the dog to go through, give him permission to pass over the threshold and out the door. His reward will be to sniff around outside for a minute. When you come back in, do the same exercise. Each time you practice, try to get the door open a little farther before permission is given and increase the time your dog has to wait. There may be times when you want him to go out immediately without waiting. This is fine, just be sure you give permission before he starts to move through the door. You do not have to be the first one through the door. Allowing the dog to exit first will not undermine your leadership role.

With a crate or car door your dog will not be on leash, so your timing will have to be faster. If the dog gets through a door without permission, you must physically bring him back to repeat the exercise. Do this calmly and with confidence.

It does not take a dog long to understand the goal of this exercise. After the first two to three times your dog has to show restraint, gradually increase the difficulty (i.e. The length of time that your dog must wait before passing through the threshold.) Remember, each time you increase the difficulty, your dog may take a step back in his training. This is normal. Stay consistent, do not verbalize your frustration, and wait for the dog to make the decision to not go through the door until he is given permission.

Allowing Pets on Furniture:

I enjoy asking my clients if they freely allow their dogs on the furniture; their looks are priceless. It reminds me of the look I would give my mother when she would note chocolate on my face, and then ask if I had been in the cookie jar.

Owners automatically assume that having their dog on the

furniture is a universal wrong. The truth is, having a dog on the furniture can be an enjoyable and relaxing experience. But, it can also foster improper behavior issues, if not done properly. You should allow your dog on the furniture, by invitation only. This will keep him from pouncing on guests or jumping up at the most, inopportune time.

If you want to prohibit your dog on any of your furniture, follow the first step of the following training method. If you want your dog on the furniture, but, only when given permission, follow all of the training method.

To eliminate a dog from being on the furniture you must not allow him access to the furniture when no one is around. This means he must be continually supervised. Jumping on furniture is a self-rewarding behavior and cannot be ignored. The first step is to interrupt the behavior with the least amount of interaction as possible. When your dog jumps on the furniture, gently remove him by slipping your fingers under his collar and guiding him off and onto the floor. Do not give a command nor utter a noise to interrupt this behavior. When he jumps back up, immediately walk over and remove him in this same gentle, but matter of fact, manner. Do not jerk the dog from the furniture; use your whole body to gently move him. The moment he is off the furniture, let go of his collar and walk away. Expect the dog to turn and jump back up onto the furniture, because he is trying to figure out why you are interrupting his behavior. After you have guided him off of the furniture, put him into a time-out. Follow the time-out procedure we talked about earlier in the book.

Follow through is important. If you begin the process of interruption you must continue until a time-out has been issued and the dog has been released. Do not have different people conducting multiple interruptions within a few minutes of each other. This will teach the dog he does not have to respect your leadership (i.e. when a father steps in to undermine a mother's authority while giving a child consequences). Whoever corrects the dog initially must follow through until the end of the exercise. For example, if your daughter puts a dog in time-out, she must be the one to release the dog from a time out. If you are the person removing the dog from furniture, you must be the one to follow though until the dog chooses to stay off the furniture, or until you release the dog from time-out. When you see your dog choosing to stay on the floor or go to his bed, give him a lot of verbal praise. Praise the behavior you do want when extinguishing one that you do not want. This training may take a week or two. After two weeks, decrease the amount of chances your dog gets before going into a time-out. More stubborn dogs will continue trying, but if you stick with it, they will eventually understand that furniture is off limits. As a matter of definition, being "on the furniture", is three or more feet, not two. If your dog attempts to stand up on the furniture using his two front feet, this is considered a jump, just ignore it because it is not self-rewarding.

To teach your dog to jump onto the furniture by invitation only, choose a specific word for that precise behavior. I use the word "couch" anytime I allow my dog on a piece of furniture. One way to reward a dog for displaying good manners (such as sitting quietly on his bed) is to reward him by allowing him onto the furniture with you. Tap the piece of furniture you want him on and say the command word. It may take your dog a minute to understand what you are asking. When the dog jumps up, praise him.

A few rules do apply once the dog is on the furniture. Do not let him sit on the back of the cushions or along the arms of the couch. He must be respectful and only get into laps of those that invite him. Once he jumps off the furniture, the invitation is no longer valid. When you are ready for furniture time to be over, use another command, such as "off," and gently remove him by the collar. Soon, your dog will begin to understand the full scope of rules surrounding furniture.

On a side note, I do not recommend allowing the dog on just one piece of furniture without permission. Having a special piece of furniture specifically for the dog is fine, but it should still be by invitation only. Remember, this dog will eventually go to his forever home and many do not want pets on any furniture.

Meeting & Greeting People/Dogs

Dogs are social creatures and love to spend time with other dogs and humans. Many dogs view time spent with either as a big reward. As a leader you control this reward.

This rule applies to dogs and people that do not live in your household and when he is on or off leash. This includes any guest that comes into your home. Teaching your dog that he is only allowed to see other dogs and people, with permission from you, will also help with the issue of "chasing", such as chasing a squirrel or deer. Teaching proper dog and human greeting is a precursor to the foundation needed to teach self-control around difficult distractions.

I see many owners walking their dog and allowing them to pull to see an approaching dog, a friendly neighbor, or to sniff a marked fire hydrant. These owners allow the leashed dog to do as they please until it becomes inconvenient. Then they correct their dog by yanking the leash and yelling inappropriately. Another problem issue that I am asked to assist with is when the owner works the dog off-leash. The owner will claim that their dog behaves well off lead, but only in a controlled environment. As soon as any distraction enters the environment, such as a person, the dog bolts to go greet him. Real life manners pertain to *all* environments. This ensures the safety of your dog and confirms your leader position. Allow your dog to be social when it is appropriate. In order for your dog to earn the right to be social, he must learn to behave appropriately.

So, what is the appropriate behavior? Self-control that does not impede your ability to communicate with another individual is appropriate behavior. Little to no barking or whining, four-feet-on-the-floor and loose leash manners are a great start. Your permission word can be the same as you use for other exercises. Anytime your dog wants to greet something and it is convenient and appropriate, wait for him to offer a positive, well-mannered behavior. When he does, verbalize the permission word and take him to the object. For instance, you are out for a walk and a see a familiar, friendly dog walking towards you. You note that your dog recognizes his friend and begins to pull towards him. Your dog pulls until they greet, and then you move on with your walk. In this instance, you may not mind that he greets his friend, but you have just allowed him to do so, without permission. You are then rewarding inappropriate behavior. A better approach would be the following. You are out for a walk and recognize that same friendly dog. Give your dog permission *before* he has the opportunity to start the inappropriate pulling behavior.

The rules are the same if someone is approaching you and your dog. If it is okay for the human to greet your dog, be sure to give your dog permission before they acknowledge, and subsequently reward any poor behavior. Again, be sure your dog is exhibiting appropriate behavior. If someone approaches your dog and he is not exhibiting good behavior (and hence, has not earned the reward to approach) then create distance from the person and relay that the dog cannot be approached. It is your responsibility to set your dog up for success. To achieve success, you cannot be shy when in public. I find it is much easier to tell people, "Sorry, my dog is in training," while taking a step back away from approaching dogs and people. People understand this, and will be appreciative.

When it is not appropriate to greet a passing dog or human, regardless of what your dog is doing, pass by without any hesitation. Create distance when needed to ensure no one rewards your dog for inappropriate behavior or before you are able to give permission. The best way to start this exercise is in a stationary position.

Stationary Exercise

The stationary exercise is a great way to teach your dog appropriate behavior when confronted with distractions of the real world. Being stationary allows you to concentrate on your dog's behavior without adding in distractions that occur while walking. If your dog cannot handle distractions when not walking, then he will never be able to handle distractions when walking whether on or off leash.

There are many places you can conduct this exercise. Start

in an area with minimal distractions such as your back yard. This will allow both you and your dog to learn at the same pace. Use a short leash, a regular or martingale collar, and a bag of mixed treats. Vary the taste quality of your dog's treats from a value of one to five.

As the leader of this exercise, you must be responsible for controlling your immediate environment. Make sure that no one reward's your dog's behavior if it is inappropriate or without permission. You are also responsible for acknowledging the good behavior that your dog is doing. This behavior may be as simple as standing quietly, or sitting nicely while another dog walks by. Look for the incremental parts of a behavior, not just the behavior as a whole. In other words, if you want your dog to sit nicely when another dog approaches, then reward when your dog first looks toward the approaching dog and does not start to lose control. As the dog gets closer, reward your dog for standing quietly. If your dog wags his tail, but does not lunge forward, reward his self-control. Do not wait for the approaching dog to walk by before you reward your dog.

A typical front yard has plenty of distractions such as squirrels, moles, rabbits, cars, children playing, dogs barking and the neighbor mowing his lawn. Your goal is to teach your dog how to react to various stimuli he encounters. You ultimately want your dog to learn what behaviors are appropriate without waiting for a command. Independent thinking will transfer to his everyday behavior in the real world. Hopefully, he will choose to forego reacting to stimuli that once, had him barking and pulling incessantly. If done correctly, your dog will choose to look to you for a reward. In the real world you want your dog to choose to leave distractions alone without waiting for a command from you.

It is critical that you have an idea as to what behavior you would like to see from your dog during these distracting moments. Before you move further with the exercise, take a moment and think about the behaviors you want to see during the following distractions...

1. As a dog passes.
2. As a human passes.
3. As a human greets your dog.
4. As a dog greets your dog.
5. As a bicycle goes by.
6. As a squirrel (cat, etc) runs by.

You must think realistically, when considering the behavior you would and would not like to see from your dog. If you expect your dog to sit every time another dog walks by, then your walks will be inefficient and boring. I recommend that you teach your dog to pass another dog without pulling, barking or lunging. If your dog learns that he cannot greet another dog without permission it will make both your lives much easier.

When working the stationary exercise prepare yourself by dressing appropriately with the appropriate shoes. Wear a soft stable shoe when doing this exercise; a pair that provides comfort and stability. Stand on a flat surface and keep your feet shoulder width apart so that you maintain strength and balance in case your dog pulls at a distraction. Be sure to create enough space between you, your dog and the distractions. Initially, start away from the road where your dog may come in contact with the distractions. The better your dog gets, the closer you can get to the distractions – such as, the sidewalk, your neighbor's fence, or a playground.

Refer back to the leash handling skills to ensure you are handling the leash appropriately. Initially, your dog will be overly excited. Stand quietly, and allow your dog to try different behaviors. Some will be inappropriate and will not receive a reward.

Allow your dog time to realize that the behavior he is offering (pulling) is not getting him any closer to the distraction, nor is it getting him the reward treat you have in your pocket. See if he offers a different behavior (barking.) If this different behavior is still a behavior you do not want, continue to ignore him. If, after a few minutes your dog does not offer an appropriate behavior (standing still for 4 seconds) and continues to offer negative behavior (twisting and jumping), put him in the house in a time-out.

If a positive behavior is exhibited (standing quiet for 4 seconds), acknowledge verbally and then reward with food. Reinforce consistently as long as the dog is offering good behavior. Once the dog is offering an appropriate behavior consistently add seconds in between each verbal acknowledgement, and intermittently disperse the food reward. If, at any time, your dog offers an inappropriate behavior, cease rewarding and ignore him. Begin the rewarding when he shows repeated good behavior.

If the appropriate behavior is consistent enough to where you are able to count to sixty, between verbal acknowledgements, then you are ready to move toward the distractions. Each movement is only one step forward. Be prepared for your dog to start pulling and lunging when you move forward. This is normal and is expected. Repeat the process; however, this time, if your dog fails to offer the appropriate behavior in the allotted time take a step backwards, instead of going back into the house for a time out. If you do back up, then the reward is verbal praise only and the opportunity to move forward again. Once forward, he earns food rewards, once again.

This exercise can be done for thirty minutes at a time, however; some dogs cannot handle thirty minutes. Do not push your dog too hard. End on a positive note by adjusting the time you work this exercise based on your dog's ability. Too many time-outs may mean you are pushing him too much.

You may not make it to the distraction zone the first time out, but you are building on the foundation. Keep in mind that each positive step forward is a move towards a dog with ingrained self-control.

This exercise will be difficult for some dogs and may take several weeks to move towards the distraction zone. Once your dog is consistent in one area, such as your front yard, go to somewhere more difficult, such as standing outside the dog park or a playground full of screaming children. The more places you go, the better your dog will become, and the faster he will adjust to unfamiliar distractions.

Object of Desire

The "object of desire" exercise is a favorite of mine. It helps dogs learn self-control around areas of high arousal. This exercise can be used for any object that your dog desires, such as the dog park, dog daycare, or going for a walk. You can also use another dog or a person as an object.

The object of desire exercise uses an increase and decrease consequence and reward schedule. Be sure to use a short leash with appropriate leash handling skills. It is imperative that your thumb stays tucked inside your pocket, so that your dog does not pull you off balance.

In order for your dog to acquire an object of his desire he must not only show self-control, but good manners as well. If your dog is like most, as soon as (if not before!) you arrive at the dog park, he is barking, whining and jumping around, in the car. This behavior will, more than likely, spill over into the park. This is a perfect opportunity to work this exercise.

Park as far away from the park entrance gate, as you can. This will provide you with plenty of opportunity to practice. Once your dog is exhibiting control for at least three seconds, put a leash on him.

Once you and your dog are outside the car, start in a stationary position. When your dog exhibits appropriate behavior, such as standing still, start to walk toward the entrance gate of the dog park. Verbalize a command that relays that you both are on the move. I use "let's go." Walk forward and continue forward until he begins to pull. When he does, back up until he is by your side, once again. Your dog does not have to be exactly by your side, but he does have to acknowledge that you are a part of the equation. Once he is with you, begin moving forward again. Repeat this process until you are close to the gate, which is the object of his desire. Then, as his reward, allow your dog to enter the park, by issuing your permission command.

During the exercise you are either moving forward or backwards. You are never stationary once you begin. The reward for being with you is the decreased distance to the object and the consequence for pulling is the distance increasing to the object. The major consequence of having to back up repeatedly is a thirty-second time-out in the car.

Do not use food during this exercise. Moving forward and reaching his object of desire is his reward. You can use limited verbal praise for the movement forward, but do not talk when you are backing up. The movement alone will communicate effectively to your dog.

If you remain patient and consistent your dog will start to pay attention to your body movement and cues, and realize that working with you gets him to the object of his desire faster than when he is out of control.

Giving and Teaching Commands

The way you give your dog commands is as important as which commands you teach. You must use a confident, but not harsh tone, and display confident body language.

If you take your dogs out in public a lot then you probably find that you give commands to him more than you do at home. When out in public you do not want to be screaming, yelling or telling your dog what to do in a firm tone. I want you to give commands as if you were sitting at a funeral.

To put yourself in your dog's position, think about being in another country where no one spoke your language. If someone tried to give you instructions in a harsh tone, in a language you did not understand, how would you feel? When dogs do not understand what you are asking of them, they can only go by your tone. When they hear your tone they typically will offer the default behavior which many times is "sit."

I often observe the following scenario in public: An owner is standing with their dog and asks him to 'sit' in a regular to firm tone. The dog knows the command, however, does not sit because he is distracted, excited or being obstinate. Two seconds later, the owner repeats it, this time, a little firmer. The dog still does not respond, so the owner changes his position, jerks up on the leash and says "sit" much firmer. This time, the dog recognizes the anger in his owner's voice so he promptly sits, an action that calms the conflict.

Three things have taken place here. The owner has taught the dog that when he is distracted, the owner is guaranteed to be inconsistent and will change the way he normally gives commands, the dog does not need to respond until the owner displays anger, and the dog does not have to respond until hearing the command several times.

Being with your dog should be fun. You should recognize first that your dog will not do everything correctly, especially during the initial training phase. He may offer inappropriate behavior, ignore your commands, and maybe embarrass you—especially in public. Lay a strong foundation in the home, and work to going into public. The more you get your dog out and the more you respond appropriately, the more consistent he will become. How quickly you get there will also depend on how you respond to his lack of inconsistency. It is okay to explain to people that your dog is in training.

Dogs are not robots and should not be treated as such. Dogs have a brain and acute senses that take in sound, smell and taste. They can be overwhelmed because of a lot of stimuli when out in public. Think about a time where you walked into a candy or candle store. Remember how all the different odors and colors flooded your senses? Dogs feel that way on a regular basis, so when you give a command it must have meaning to your dog so it pushes through the other stimuli so he can respond appropriately. This does not happen immediately. The speed in which it takes place will depend on your dog's maturity level, level of self-control and experience.

As your dog matures and gains experience, the times you may have to ask him to do something will dramatically decrease. As a rule, you should only have to tell your dog to do something a maximum of two times. Preferably, we only want to tell them once, but reality means you may have to repeat *after* you give the dog a chance to respond.

When giving a command you want to use a normal tone of voice or less. Even during the times you may have to raise your volume due to distance, do not use harsh or firm tones. When giving a command give it in a confident manner. Do not drag the word out but say it short and concise and do not repeat. Once you give the command, count to five silently to yourself; this allows your dog an opportunity to receive the command, process it and respond. After five seconds, you may ask the dog again using the same normal tone you used the first time you asked.

Get out of the habit of constantly repeating commands to your dog. Practice whispering commands and work up to a normal tone of voice. Practice counting five silently to yourself and then repeat the command the same way. Once you feel comfortable, practice giving your dog commands this way. Be sure to only use commands he knows solidly.

Owners typically rush to put commands with behaviors. I encourage owners to focus on acknowledging the behavior they want to see repeated and then make a decision as to what word they want to associate it with, if any. Many behaviors that I encourage owners to reward do not have a command such as playing with a toy, chewing on a bone, quietly watching neighbors work in their yard or observing quietly during family dinner. The behaviors that need to be named are behaviors you will need the dog to do during specific circumstances such as staying in one place, leaving a dead animal alone or coming when called.

When you think about the behaviors you want to put on

command, take some things into consideration. Are the commands going to be easy to remember and natural to use? Which language would you prefer? If you are fostering a dog and working to put commands with desirable behaviors, I recommend using English.

Put together a list of commands for particular behaviors so there is consistency throughout your household. If you are fostering a dog, give this list to the family adopting your foster dog.

Here are commands I commonly use:

Sit—"Sit"

Lying Down—"Down"

Getting off Furniture—"Off"

Coming—"Come"

Walking Nicely on Leash—"With me"

Stay—"Stay"

Leaving an Object Alone—"Leave It"

Permission Word—"Okay"

Getting in the Car—"Load Up"

Getting in the Crate—"Crate"

Lying Down on a Bed—"Bed"

Permission to get on Furniture—"Couch"

Look at Me—The dog's name

Your list may be longer and should contain every behavior you want to put on command, including tricks. Be sure everyone in the household is using the same commands so the dog is not confused and frustrated.

Dogs do not understand our language but they do learn to associate certain words with different actions, and can also learn body language and hand signals. If you choose to do hand signals, mix them with the oral commands and add them to your list.

Once you have marked a behavior consistently and your dog understands that offering that behavior earns a reward, you can put a command with it. Continue to mark the behavior just as you have been but now you will time the behavior with the command. Here is how to do this properly:

1. You see your dog about to put his rear-end on the floor. *During* the action, say the command for "sit."

2. Once your dog completes the behavior, acknowledge

and reward as before.

3. While you are rewarding your dog, feel free to repeat the command only to give your dog another opportunity to hear it. You are not saying it at this point to get him to comply.

It will take many repetitions to get your dog to understand the command. Remember that you can associate a word with any behavior your dog offers consistently. Any time you see your dog about to offer the behavior, say the command and reward when he completes it. You can also acknowledge the dog for a behavior and put the word in the acknowledgement. If you walk in the room and your dog sits before you are able to say the command, acknowledge with a "good boy, good sit." This way, he is hearing the command in the acknowledgement.

Once you think your dog understands the command you need to test it. Testing should occur at a different time than the association exercise. Give the command before your dog does the behavior and wait at least five seconds to see if he responds. If he does not respond within five seconds then he probably does not have the association and you need to go back to that step. The faster he responds the better he understands.

If your dog is consistently responding to a command, it is time to change the way you reward it. This process teaches your dog that he must listen to your command to earn the reward and not just offer the behavior when convenient. When the behavior is offered without a command, still acknowledge it, but do not offer a food reward. Food rewards will now only come when the dog responds to a command within five seconds. You can also start shaping the behavior to get your dog to respond faster. Reward with food if the dog does it before the five seconds has ended then require four seconds, three seconds, etc. Each step will need to be rewarded several times over before expecting him to do it faster.

Your final step to teaching the command is to vary the reward. This will take place once the dog is consistently responding to your command. The varying of the reward will now take place whether you ask your dog to do a behavior or if he offers it randomly. Consider yourself a slot machine. You want your dog to "pull the lever" over and over again to see if he can win. The variable reinforcement schedule will cause the behavior to be stronger and more likely to occur.

If you are positive your dog understands a command, but will not offer it after five seconds, try again. If he still will not offer the behavior after another five seconds, put him in time-out for thirty seconds.

Your dog may respond well in a controlled environment but when you are in public the distractions may get in the way. Instead of responding quickly he may take a few seconds longer, which is very natural. If he knows the command consistently then you can begin to put the two-command rule in place. Whatever you do, do not change your behavior by changing your tone, your position or physically touching the dog to get him to respond. Reward with food the first several times your dog responds out in public.

Some dogs learn faster than others, so be patient. The more commands you teach your dog the faster he will respond. I recommend teaching commands for good manners and some fun tricks he can use to charm his adopting potential family.

"Leave It"

"Leave it" is one of the most useful commands you can teach your dog. This command is especially useful for situations you are unable to train for such as rolling in a dead animal, licking the lotion off your legs, or eating deer feces.

The behavior you are looking for when giving your dog this command is for your dog to take his attention away from something. If he is staring at something he should look away, if he has something in his mouth he should drop it, if he is standing near something he should walk away.

Use food to start teaching this behavior. Once you teach the command you will begin generalizing it with other items. The key during teaching is always to have something more rewarding than what you are asking the dog to leave alone.

The final rule to this command is the dog should never earn the object you are asking him to leave. For example, do not use this command to ask your dog to leave his food alone until you are ready to give him permission, because essentially he will be earning what you told him to leave alone.

To begin, get a "mediocre" treat small enough to fit in between two fingers; your dog should not be able to access it. This will be the treat your dog is going to "leave" in order to earn something better. Sit somewhere isolated with your dog. Place the mediocre treat between your fingers and do not say anything. Do not put the treat in his face, just in a position to where he can reach it. He will begin mouthing, licking and nibbling to try and get to the treat. Keep your hand still and say nothing. He will eventually see that what he is trying is not working. When he pulls back, verbally mark the behavior and give him a better treat. Do not pull the mediocre treat away until after you have verbally marked the behavior and are ready to give him the better treat. If your dog chooses to not lick the treat at all after a few attempts, verbally mark and reward. Do not wait for your dog to touch the forbidden object. There will be times when you want your dog to leave something alone before he puts his mouth on it, like a dead animal. Once he understands the game, move the forbidden treat to another location.

Depending on the size of your dog you can place the treat on your knee or the floor. No matter where you place the treat, be sure to keep a finger on top of it so the dog is unable to get to it. He will attempt to get the treat the way he did before. Wait until he pulls away, and then verbally mark the behavior and reward. Again, do not move the forbidden treat away until *after* you have verbally marked the correct behavior. Keep making the game harder so your dog understands the game is about leaving the object alone.

To make the game more difficult, place the forbidden treat on the floor and remove your hand. If your dog goes for it, cover it up without saying anything. As soon as your dog pulls away, remove your hand and see if he continues to leave it alone. Cover it up as many times as you need. When he chooses to leave it alone for at least three seconds verbally mark it and reward with something better. This is more challenging for your dog but also more realistic.

You are now ready to begin practicing dropping the treat. When you begin to drop the forbidden treat, be sure your hand is close enough to cover it up if your dog goes for it. Do not verbally interrupt your dog during this exercise. Work this part until you are able to drop the forbidden treat from high up without your dog going for it and without you staring at him. Make it as realistic as possible.

When your dog is consistently leaving the forbidden treat alone whether in your hand or dropped on the floor, begin associating the command.

Place the treat back between your fingers and hold it out for your dog. As soon as your dog acknowledges you have a treat, give the command for "leave it" and allow the dog to respond. When he responds by pulling away, verbally mark and reward. Practice each step several times before moving forward. By the time you get to dropping the treat on the floor your dog should understand the association between the command and the behavior.

When your dog is consistent with this exercise you can begin generalizing with other objects. Set up an exercise outside on leash with your dog. Be sure to have treats in your pocket. Take him for a short walk and allow him to stop and sniff objects. After he has sniffed for a few seconds, calmly say the command and wait for him to respond. As soon as he does, verbally mark and reward. Do this with many different objects. Do not wait until you really need him to leave something alone before practicing.

If your dog is being consistent over a couple of weeks, start rewarding on a variable schedule. There will be times where he earns a yummy reward when leaving something alone and other times he just earns praise. This is also when you will start using interruptions and consequences for not responding. Give your dog five seconds to respond before repeating the command. If he does not respond within five seconds, physically interrupt him. You can use either the split up technique or you can move him by the collar. If you physically have to remove him using either technique, initiate a time-out. The time-out may be on a leash next to you or isolated away from the object depending on the situation. If he goes back to the forbidden object, repeat the process.

If you must do a lot of time-outs you may have rushed the exercise. Go back a couple of steps and ensure he understands what you are asking of him. Stay consistent; if you ask him to leave something alone be sure he follows through.

Sit & Down

These two behaviors are considered part of basic obedience and will often be the first couple of behaviors rewarded. These are easy behaviors to capture, reward and name as dogs do them naturally. Dogs give owners many opportunities to acknowledge these behaviors without any effort on the owner's part. Think about how many times during the day you see your dog sit or lay down. Because these two behaviors occur naturally there is no need to lure a dog into doing them. Luring just adds an extra step that will have to be eliminated later.

If you reward "sit" and "down" your dog will list it as something he can do to earn something he wants. He will begin to exhibit the behaviors on a regular basis for attention, toys, interaction and food. To put these on command just follow the steps mentioned above.

Jumping

Jumping is one of the most common inappropriate behaviors I see. Do not allow your dog to jump as an offered behavior.

Jumping occurs when a dog is jumping up on a human, a door, a gate, a fence, or when placing two feet on a chair.

Dogs do not jump in order to establish dominance or to get closer to your face. They jump because it is natural and it receives some sort of acknowledgement from humans.

Many people try to remedy jumping by holding the dog's paws, kneeing him in the chest, smacking him on the nose, grabbing him by the collar or giving a command. All these actions are giving the dog attention or are placing fear into the dog for offering a behavior.

Ignoring is very powerful and can be used to eliminate many behaviors that are not self-rewarding. If we ignore the jumping we can teach the dog that it is not a desired behavior. Owners have a harder time ignoring this behavior because many times it is uncomfortable or it happens to guest in the home that does not know to ignore.

Ignoring means you do not look at, touch or talk to your

dog. Avoid eye contact with him and turn away if you must. When your dog realizes the behavior is not getting him attention, he will offer something else. When he offers an appropriate behavior for at least three seconds verbally mark and reward. If you acknowledge too quickly, you will teach him a chained behavior. Reward as long as he has four-on-the-floor. If at any time he begins jumping again, ignore.

If your dog jumps on you to throw a toy, simply ignore and wait for the appropriate behavior before throwing. He does not have to sit but needs to have all four feet on the ground.

When faced with other humans that want to greet your dog you must take responsibility in setting him up for success; especially if you plan on taking your foster to adoption events or out in public for training.

Because you cannot trust other people to know your dog is in training, you must control your dog's immediate environment. This means limiting your dog's options and controlling the response of others. Place your dog on a leash. Allow your dog to greet people with permission. If your dog exhibits appropriate behavior, praise him exuberantly; however, if he jumps, take a step back. This is an interruption with little interaction. Once the dog is giving appropriate behavior, give permission and allow him to greet the person again. Do not assume another person will ignore your dog when he jumps.

Loose Leash Walking

Another common complaint from owners is that their dog pulls on leash. Unfortunately, not many rescue dogs get the opportunity to be on a leash. If they have been housed in a shelter their walks on leash may not have been regular.

I encourage you to stay away from training tools such as a head collar or a correction collar. A regular flat or martingale collar will work just fine. Do not use retractable leashes as they are not conducive to teaching loose lead walking.

First, practice stationary exercises with your dog. When your dog is comfortable with this, move to the object of desire exercises.

The last exercise you will use is the change of direction exercise. Start somewhere easy for your dog such as the backyard or the driveway. You may use food rewards but keep them in your pocket on the opposite side of your dog until you need to reward. Do not use the food as a lure. Begin walking by saying "let's go." If your dog is walking nicely verbalize and reward. Try not to stop walking while rewarding him. The moment your dog starts to pull, turn away from him and walk in the opposite direction. Do not let your hand slip from your pocket. When he is walking nicely with you for a minimum of three steps verbalize and reward. Use small treats so he does not need to stop and chew. This exercise will encourage him to keep an eye on the human but still be aware of where he is going. As you practice require the dog to take more steps with you before earning the reward.

If your dog attempts to cross behind you, continue forward until he adjusts. Do not use the leash to pull him back to the appropriate side. If he attempts to cross in front of you slow down your walking and shuffle your steps until he adjusts back to the appropriate side.

Stay

Teaching "stay" for real life situations means you place your dog in the stay position, and he stays there, without you having to keep an eye on him, or back away slowly. There are many instances in your daily routine or extracurricular activities where your dog will need to stay in the same place for an extended amount of time.

A client of mine found that teaching her dog this command with real life expectations was important one day while she was hiking with her dog. She came upon a man that had wrecked his bicycle. He was sitting on the ground and was very disoriented. She placed her dog in an off-leash stay about ten feet from where the man sat, and moved to take care of him. The man ended up having a head injury that required her to call for an ambulance and get in touch with his wife. Ten minutes later she remembered that she had put her dog in a stay. Even with all the commotion and distractions, her dog was still in the same place waiting for a release from her owner.

"Stay" should mean that your dog stays in a certain spot until you, or whoever put him in position, releases him. "Stay" means the dog should not move from a certain *spot,* not a certain area. If you want your dog to stay in a certain area find another word that you would like to associate such as "wait." Do not repeat the command over and over again while staring at the dog.

I integrate a hand signal with this command. You may find that there are times you need to place your dog into a stay and are unable to give an audible verbal command because of the environment. Use an open-hand with palm facing the dog. You do not have to place your hand directly in front of your dog's face. You will not always be close enough to do so.

Do not be predictable when releasing your dog. For example, you do not want your dog to think you are releasing him every time you turn to face him. Release your dog when your back is turned to him, when facing him, turned sideways and even when walking back to him. He needs to learn to listen to the command and not read your body. I use "okay" as the release word. If you place him in a stay do not give him another command such as "come" until after you have given him the release command.

When you release your dog from his stay be sure he moves to receive his reward. By having him move you are helping him understand what his release word means. He does not have to move far in order to receive his reward.

Put together a bag of treats, just small enough to taste. You may place these on a counter nearby or in your pocket or training pouch. Ask your dog to "sit" or "down," and praise him when he does. Place your hand up, with palm facing the dog and say the word "stay." Turn sideways from your dog for a second and then release. Take a step back and reward your dog. You may toss the reward on the floor or make him take it from your hand, either way he must move at least a step to receive it. Repeat the process. Slowly start turning more away from the dog and adding a little distance. When you add distance you do not have to add time. He may be able to stay for ten seconds with you standing next to him with your back turned, but when you take a step away he may only be able to stay for one second; this is normal. If at any time your dog moves out of his stay, place him back in the exact spot and ask for it again. If he breaks the stay regularly you may have moved too quickly and will need to take a few steps back and do some easy ones. Again, do not be predictable when teaching this behavior; do not have a routine. Sometimes work short distance with long duration and then change it to long distance with short duration. The key is to help the dog understand that when you give him the "stay" command you want him to do nothing but wait for the release.

Start this exercise in the house before taking it outside. When you take it outside I recommend you place the dog on a long leash if he does not come when called or if he tends to play "catch me if you can." When you start outside or with distractions, go back to something easy and let him win. The more he wins, the more he will learn.

Coming When Called

Having a dog that comes when called can literally save his life because it can keep him from running into dangerous situations. In order to teach a successful "come" command you must have an idea of what you expect from your dog.

"Come" is the act of the dog moving in your direction, not coming to you and sitting. By requiring your dog to come to you and sit before earning a reward, you are rewarding the "sit" behavior, not the "come." If you would like your dog to sit at the end of a "come," make sure he knows the "come" command, reward that, *then* ask your dog to sit.

Give you dog the "come" command. When he comes to you, gently grab his collar, pet him and give him a treat. Then, give him a release word. You want to teach your dog that coming to you yields rewards, and that he is not to move again until you give him a release. Verbally reward your dog as he moves toward you. As the dog progresses in learning this command, require him to come closer before earning a verbal reward.

Anytime your dog comes to you on his own verbally mark it and reward. He will start to learn that you are fun to visit and sometimes will just check in with you to see if you will dispense treats or praise.

Always work the "stay" and "come" commands separately until your dog understands both. Use a 30' cotton leash while teaching this exercise. Start working in the backyard allowing the dog to roam freely with the leash attached; be sure the handle of the leash is in your hand so it does not get caught on anything. Call your dog by name and give the command with enthusiasm. If your dog has never heard of the word "come" before then use some excitability and clapping. You want the dog to see you as a "party." You will find that children have no problem working this exercise. As your dog turns and begins to head in your direction, say the word "come" and then verbally praise. When your dog reaches you, gently get him by the collar (do not pull him towards you), pet him and give him a bite of treat. Do not get the treat out of your pocket until you have him by the collar. Once he eats his treat, give him the release command.

If your dog does not come when you begin throwing your "party," *gently* begin to reel him in with the leash. Do not jerk your dog towards you. You may continue calling him while doing this. If he begins to come on his own at any time, stop reeling and begin verbally marking the behavior. Do this repeatedly until he starts to understand what is expected of him. Begin to change the distance your dog is from you when you call him. Sometimes, call your dog back immediately after you have released him to help him understand that "turning on a dime" when called is preferred.

Once your dog begins to understand what you expect, you will add consequences and greater expectations. Begin requiring a faster response while on leash. A faster response means a better treat and less time before receiving a release word. The longer it takes your dog to respond the less you treat, and the longer he has to stay with you before getting released.

If you get a lot of slow responses or have to reel him in several times, implement a time-out and then go out and try again.

You will work off-leash in a similar fashion. Call your dog to you. If he does not come, take a step or two towards him and call again. Do this until he chooses to come toward you. The second he turns to come to you verbally praise and finish the sequence all the way to the release. If you find that you have to walk all the way to him before he responds many times go back to on-leash work. Implement time-outs when your dog understands the command and is doing it consistently. Once you release him from the time-out call him quickly to give him a chance to respond appropriately. Each successful "come" must earn praise and/or food.

Physically go get your dog if you do not have time to follow-through with the command. Do not give a verbal command. Always praise your dog for allowing you to approach him so he sees it as a positive experience.

Excessive Barking

Barking is a natural form of communication for dogs. They use barking to warn of danger, warn of other dogs and people in their territory, from excitement and as an offered behavior to get attention or other rewards. You should never attempt to eliminate barking or make a dog afraid to bark, but you do need to teach a "quiet" command to help control it. A dog that stands at the window and barks at everything that moves outside is sure to not stay in a home very long. An incessant barker can be a nuisance to neighbors, friends and family and other dogs.Barking can be both self-rewarding and non-self-rewarding. If the dog is barking at you to get something then ignore it, but if he is barking at something outside to get it to move away then consider it a self-rewarding behavior, and you must interrupt that behavior.

To interrupt incessant or inappropriate barking, use the split-up technique. When your dog is barking at a window, use the split-up to redirect him. Confidently walk between your dog and the window. Walk toward your dog until he redirects. As you do the technique, use the command "that's enough." The moment he walks away, do so as well. He is allowed to return to the window as long as he is quiet. Verbally praise him when he is quiet at the window, and reiterate the "that's enough" command by saying "good 'that's enough.'"

If you have to use the split-up technique three times, put your dog into time-out.

This technique can be used any time you need to interrupt your dog for barking. You can use it for barking out the window, at the cat, another dog or a person. The person being barked at cannot implement this technique but should just ignore.

A dog that barks in the crate is another problem that is difficult for owners. Dogs bark in their crates either because they need to go outside, or because they want to play. Either way, you cannot interrupt the behavior without giving the dog attention. Walking into a room where a dog is barking from his crate is rewarding the behavior even if you do not let him out. Talking to him from another room is also rewarding. Ignoring is the most powerful technique to use with this but you must follow through. Do not ignore for ten minutes and then suddenly scream at the dog; otherwise you are teaching him to bark for longer periods to get your attention. I recommend placing the crate somewhere away from the family where the barking is less audible. I also encourage you to bake cookies or buy gift cards if you have neighbors that might complain about the noise. Most neighbors are satisfied if they know you are working on the problem.

Do not allow your dog to bark to tell you he wants to go out and potty, to get out of the crate, to get a treat, during dinner prep time, to come inside or to get you to answer the front door when someone is there. Be aware of when the dog is using barking as an offered behavior and how you can stop rewarding it. Most importantly, verbally acknowledge him when he is quiet.

Prey Drive

Every dog has prey and hunt drive though not all dogs prey on the same thing. Some dogs may also have a higher prey drive than others. Your Labrador may love to chase a ball, but could care less about chasing a deer or a cat. This is because he finds chasing the ball more rewarding than chasing an animal since they always catch the ball but not the animal.

Dogs that chase moving objects, especially wild animals and cats, can find themselves in rescues and shelters because they become lost or because the owner does not know how to remedy the behavior. There are things that we can do to help curb this behavior and teach a new behavior to take its place.

Teaching self-control will help with this issue tremendously. By teaching your dog he cannot have a desired object unless given permission, you will help teach him to not chase things such as deer, squirrels, rabbits or the family cat.

Start out by placing a tennis ball in your hand. Hold the ball out to your dog with your hand covering it as much as possible. When the dog tries to go for the ball, gently move the ball away, but only as far as you have to move it; do not put the ball above your head or behind your back. Stay quiet when doing this technique. Moving the ball slightly away when your dog tries to grab it communicates much more than using any type of negative word. When he backs away, place the ball back into the starting position. Repeat as necessary until your dog stops attempting to take the ball. When the ball is in the starting position and your dog is not going for it, tell him "okay" and give him the ball. You are teaching your dog that grabbing for the ball does not work, but when given permission he is welcome to have the desired object.

Once he understands this exercise, start tossing the ball up and down in front of your dog. Toss it just a few inches up away from your hand. When your dog tries to go for it stop tossing and move the ball slightly away if he attempts to grab it. Once your dog understands to leave the tossed ball alone, give him permission, "okay," and then toss it to him.

When the dog starts understanding this concept I start making it more difficult. I like to really get happy with the ball tossing and I will begin to take my attention away from him; not giving him eye contact. I will toss it back and forth from hand to hand and I will often do this very close to the dog. When the dog is doing well, (he does not have to do it for a long period of time), I will throw the ball and give permission to go after it. I never throw a ball for a dog to chase without giving permission to the dog to chase it; even if that is the game I am playing and I am not working on self-control specifically with the techniques discussed above.

Next, hook your dog to a short leash. Toss the ball a few feet away with one hand while holding the leash with the other. If your dog starts to exhibit inappropriate behavior such as barking, lunging, pulling or whining, ignore him. Do not pull back on the leash and do not correct him. When the dog is exhibiting controlled excitement, unhook the leash and give the dog permission to go and get the ball. Do this many times until you can do this without the dog being leashed. If your dog goes after the ball without permission while off-leash, you must go and get him, bring him back to the original spot and do it again. Leave the ball where it was tossed. If the dog picks up the ball, take it from him, put it back and start over.

Cat chasing in the home is a common problem and often results in the dog being rehomed or the cat being banned to a separate room until the dog is isolated. Cat chasing is not always the result of a high prey drive. Cat chasing can be a fun and entertaining game to a dog, especially if he has played with cats before. A cat that runs from a dog rewards the dog's behavior.

To work on this issue, leash your dog and sit in an area that is conducive to teaching. Have treats available and out of the dog's sight. When your cat crosses in front of your dog, reward him with verbal praise and a treat if he displays calm behavior, and is not barking or lunging at the cat. If someone is helping you by holding the cat, be sure to keep plenty of distance between your dog and cat, so your helper does not get scratched.

Off-leash work will start in the same position. Bring the cat in (either alone or with a helper holding him), if it is tolerant of the dog being close, and allow the dog off-leash. As soon as you let the dog off-leash, give him permission to go and see the cat. Allow your dog to go up to the cat. If he is exhibiting appropriate behavior such as sniffing, verbally praise and give a treat. We want to make sure he understands that being nice to the cat is more rewarding than chasing the cat. If your dog offers inappropriate behavior, hook him to the leash and sit back down for thirty seconds. After thirty seconds, repeat the process.

This can be used with squirrels, rabbits and deer. When working with wild animals it will take a little longer since you do not have control over wild creatures. Be patient and work in short sessions. Be sure to have treats at hand. Make the exercise more difficult, by using a long leash, (not a retractable on). This will allow him to make choices running away from you.

CHAPTER 9
COMMON PUPPY PROBLEMS

If a solid manners foundation is not started when a dog is young, common problems such as mouthing, chewing and housebreaking will persist through adulthood. I believe many dogs end up in rescues because owners think the dog will grow out of these behaviors. If chewing on the leg of a table is a stress reliever and offers the dog stimulation, he is not going to stop just because he is considered an adult.

While it is easier to lay a foundation for puppies because they have not yet been rewarded for bad behavior, it is important to understand that dogs are never too old to learn new behaviors and manners. With knowledge and consistency, it is easy to teach dogs the proper skills to move them past a puppy mentality.

Crate Training:

Some owners see crates as cruel and inhumane, while others see it as a saving grace. I believe the latter. Crates are a great way to set a dog up for success, especially when they cannot be supervised. Crate training helps dogs with housebreaking and chewing and offers them security.

Many dogs in rescues have either never been crated or

have been crated too much. You first need to ensure there are positive associations with the crate. This will allow to further teach appropriate skills that will helps dogs be more successful in their forever homes.

First, choose the correct crate for the dog you are teaching. Ensure the crate is large enough for the dog to stand up and turn around in. The crate should not be too large as many dogs will eliminate in one corner, and sleep in another. Plastic crates are best for dogs that may be destructive or are escape artists. Wire crates work great for dogs who are fearful or for dogs who have accidents while crated. Mesh crates work best for dogs that are comfortable being crated, and are great in a car.

Next, introduce a reward when the dog enters the crate. Get some high value rewards such as hamburger, chicken or something the dog does not get on a regular basis. Put the shortest leash possible on the dog or hold the dog gently by the collar. Stand in front of the crate with the dog and do not allow him to move away. He can attempt to move away, but he will be limited. Stay quiet and wait for the dog to move one foot towards the crate. When he does, verbally mark and give a reward. Do not use the reward as a bribe or a lure by having the dog follow the treat into the crate. Next, wait for the dog to offer two paws before earning the reward and so on. Once the dog has all four paws in the crate, give the dog a Kong filled with treats and close the door. Leave the dog in for a minute and then allow the dog to come out. Be sure you pick up the Kong and put it away. Start the process over with one paw and so on, until the dog enters the crate. After a few repetitions you will wait until the dog gets two paws in the crate before giving a reward, eventually requiring all four paws to earn the reward and the Kong. If you have a small dog, you may physically place the dog in the crate and then offer the Kong.

Only allow a dog to have the Kong toy while in the crate. If we allow him to have the Kong outside of the crate, it loses its power.

Another technique you can use for dogs that are uncomfortable with crating is to leave the door open allowing your dog to explore the crate on his own. Each time you notice him interested verbally mark the behavior and reward with a high value treat. Once he is consistently going into the crate, offer the Kong and close the door. Wait a couple of minutes and let your dog out of the crate. Be sure you put the Kong away and only allow him to have it when in the crate. Do this exercise several times a day before you need to keep your dog contained for longer periods.

If your dog is okay going into the crate but does not do well once contained, we can still use the Kong. Once the dog is in the crate, give him the Kong. After a couple of minutes with the door closed, let the dog out and put the Kong away. Each time you put the dog in the crate he gets the Kong. Increase the time in the crate slowly. If your dog is whining, barking or crying in the crate, ignore it completely. Never let a crying, whining or barking dog out of a crate. Require quiet for at least three seconds before acknowledging the dog and moving to let him out.

Dogs with intense anxiety when crated can harm themselves. If this is true of your dog, find another place to isolate the dog such as a laundry room or a bathroom; somewhere the dog can be safe from harm. I recommend speaking with your veterinarian about some calming medication while you work through these issues.

Dogs that have been placed in a crate for extended periods of time often get in the habit of eliminating in the space on themselves. To help dogs overcome this issue, remove all towels or blankets from the crate. Blankets and towels will only soak up urine in the crate. Begin feeding the dog off the bottom of a cleaned crate without a bowl. This will help him associate the bottom of the crate with food instead of elimination. Working on housebreaking issues outside the crate is important in this exercise as well.

Not every dog needs to be trained to be in a crate. If you have a dog that does not need to be isolated in a crate then do not stress getting the dog trained in this area. Work on other issues instead.

Housebreaking:

Housebreaking is a common problem among many dogs regardless of their history. Housebreaking a dog can be one of the most frustrating behaviors to work on and will take some time.

Dogs are all about substrate preference. Whatever their paws are on when they eliminate will be where they learn to eliminate. For example, if a dog is raised in a concrete run, then concrete will be his preferred "potty." Regardless of where the dog was raised, you can help him learn the appropriate place to eliminate is outdoors. I do not recommend litter box training or paper training, even for small dogs, as this teaches the dog to eliminate inside the home.

The steps for housebreaking are the same whether the dog is 7 weeks, 7 months or 7 years. The difference is the physiological capability that comes with age. It takes a lot of patience, true commitment and attention to detail on your part.

There are three steps to housebreaking a dog. The first step is teaching the dog that the preferred area to eliminate is grass, the second step is teaching the dog how to tell you he needs to eliminate, and the third step is teaching the dog how to hold it for a period of time without eliminating indoors.

To teach a dog that grass is the only place to eliminate, ensure you are taking the dog to the grass regularly. When the dog eliminates in the grass, give a reward and lots of praise. Supervision is the key to being successful with housebreaking. I recommend the use of a crate when you are unable to supervise your dog. If the dog does not do well in a crate or you do not want them to be in the crate, attach a leash to him and to yourself so you always know where the dog is. Without supervision, the dog can easily slip away and potty without your knowledge. Each time the dog eliminates somewhere other than the substrate preference you take a step back. If you do catch your dog relieving himself inside, simply distract him by clapping, and immediately take him outside. Again, reward when the dog eliminates outside. Do not yell or run at a dog that is using the bathroom inside. This will cause the dog to become afraid to eliminate in front of people, causing him to hide "surprises" throughout the house.

Teaching a dog how to tell you they need to potty is as easy as ringing a bell. Hang a bell on a door low enough for the dog to reach. The bell needs to be loud enough to hear throughout the house. Each time you take the dog out, ask if he needs to go outside, take him to the door and ring the bell. Immediately open the door and go outside to his "potty" spot. After doing this for a week you will then allow your dog a chance to ring the bell on his own. Take him to the door and ask him if he needs to go potty and then wait. Give your dog a chance to touch the bell either with his nose or his paw. At this point, you are not waiting for a loud ring, just an acknowledgement that the dog understands the association between going out to potty and the bell. If he touches, verbally mark and then immediately take him outside to his potty spot. You will do this each time you take him out to potty. Most dogs will pick this up rather quickly.

The final step is teaching a dog how to "hold it" for longer periods of time. Except for puppies, most dogs do well holding it overnight. This is because there are fewer stimuli during the night (i.e. noises, physical activity, food and water). Puppies' bladders are much smaller and not as developed as older dogs, so they will need to go outside more often during the day. A basic guide for knowing how long a puppy can hold his bladder is by taking the puppy's monthly age and adding an hour, (for instance, a 3-month-old puppy should be able to go 4 hours without going outside). Use this only as a guide, as your dog may not be able to hold it as long until it is more developed and understands your expectations. Also take into consideration the size of your dog. If you have a small dog, it may have to go out more often than a larger dog. Write down how frequently you typically take your dog outside. If it is every 2 hours, start increasing that time to every 2½ hours. When owners get new dogs, especially puppies, they tend to take the dog out too often; never giving him a chance to learn how to hold it. You must begin to increase the time each day requiring him to hold it longer each time. How much you increase the time will depend on each individual dog.

When housebreaking, do not allow the dog to use a doggie door, and always go out with the dog during elimination time so you are able to reward the behavior. One of the biggest mistakes owners make with housebreaking is they put the dog out for an hour and then bring him in without knowing if he eliminated. Allowing a dog access to the yard through a doggie door also teaches the dog he can go whenever he wants, which does not teach him to hold it for longer periods of time.

The schedule I have provided is based on the needs of a puppy, however, you can modify it based on your dog's age and size, and your lifestyle.

You take your dog out:

> First thing in the morning
> 20-30 minutes after eating
> After rambunctious play
> After waking from a nap
> After being let out of the crate
> Every 30-45 minutes during the day and evening when you are home.
> Overnight, new puppies will need to go outside between 3-5 hours after bedtime.

Let's look at an average schedule for a new puppy where the entire family is gone during the day:

5:30am-Dog goes outside on leash and with treats. Dog should urinate and may have to defecate. Reward the dog with a treat immediately after he eliminates.

5:45am-Dog eats breakfast. You may use the regular or hand-feeding technique in the mornings with puppies.

5:50am-Take dog outside immediately after eating, on leash for another potty break. If the dog is older you may be able to wait thirty minutes.

6:00am-Family plays and trains dog stimulating him for his morning exercise.

6:10am-Dog will need to eliminate again due to the stimulation.

6:20am-Dog comes back in, plays some more until family is ready to leave for the day.

6:45am-Dog needs to be taken outside for one final potty break until lunch.

7:00am-Dog is put into crate with a toy full of peanut butter, a small bowl with an ice cube and a toy.

11:00am-Dog walker or family member comes home to let the dog out to potty and to eat lunch. Dog is immediately taken outside. Do not interact with the dog until dog has eliminated. Dog may not have to poop at this time. You will learn your dog's routine over a week or two.

11:15am-Dog is fed lunch.

11:30am-Dog is taken back outside for potty break.

11:35am-Interact and play with the dog.

11:45am-Dog is taken outside for final lunch potty. Dog will need to defecate at this time.

12:00pm-Dog is put back into crate until family arrives at home in the afternoon.

4:00pm-Dog is immediately taken outside without any interaction from family until dog has eliminated.

4:15pm-Dog is brought back inside for supervised play

4:30pm-Stop play, take outside for elimination. Bring in for supervised play, taking out every 30-45 minutes.

6:00pm-Feed dinner. This is a good time to feed using the hand-feeding technique.

6:30pm-Outside for elimination

6:30pm-Supervised play; take out every 30-45 minutes until bedtime.

During the overnight hours your dog should hold it longer due to a lack of stimulation. I would start with every three hours and increase as the week goes by.

Do:

-Get yourself and the puppy on a schedule.
-Add 3-5 minutes to time the dog must wait throughout the week.
-Treat the dog every time it potties outside. Do this outside.
-Take the dog out on a leash.
-Ring the bell every time you take the dog outside.
-Supervise your dog at all times when outside or inside the house.
-Be consistent.
-Learn your particular dog's schedule.

Do not:

-Wait for the dog to ask before taking him outside. He's not ready for that step.

-Punish the dog for going in the house.

-Wait for the dog to wake up in the middle of the night and cry before you take outside.

-Allow your dog free run inside the house for the first couple of weeks.

-Allow your dog to roam free if he did not do his business outside.

-Allow your dog to be gated unsupervised in an area larger than his crate.

-Use a doggie door until the dog is housebroken.

-Use puppy pads inside the home.

Mouthing:

Mouthing is a common problem with puppies and adults alike. Not matter the age a dog needs to learn never to place his teeth on human skin.

Dogs naturally play using their mouths, however they can learn bite inhibition. They learn this with other dogs and they can learn it with you through the use of dog language.

When a dog bites during play, you may react by yelling or swatting the dog. This does not teach the dog that biting hurts, it only teaches that we are unpredictable. Using words such as 'no bite' and 'easy' will not teach them either.

A dog will let out a quick, high-pitched yelp and pull himself away from another dog if play becomes too rough; he will then ignore the dog for a few seconds before deciding if he wants to continue playing. You can use this method to educate your dog on proper play skills with you. The next time your dog nips you, give a high-pitched yelp, pull away as if you have touched a hot stove, and ignore the dog for at least five seconds. Remember that ignoring means you do not acknowledge the dog in any way. After five seconds you may give your dog attention again. Remember to praise if he is not biting.

Practice yelping away from the dog so he does not get immune to it; and do not worry if your yelp does not mimic a dog's exactly. Just ensure you yelp (showing pain), pull away and ignore.

There will be moments when the first yelp does not work because the dog is too hyperactive. Do not change your method, just give him another yelp with the pull away and ignore. If you have to do this three times in a row, put your dog into a time-out. After a week of giving three strikes, go to two strikes and then one strike. Giving your dog lots of play dates with other dogs will also help the process go more quickly.

CHAPTER 10
BEHAVIOR PROBLEMS

Unlike manner problems, behavior problems are deep-rooted issues that stem from a lack of a basic need and/or confidence. Fear, anxiety, aggression, and resource guarding are just a few behavior issues that plague many of today's canines. Dogs that end up in rescues typically have one or more behavior issues. Many foster parents and rescue organizations have no experience in dealing with serious behavior problems, and dogs can spend months or years in a foster home before adoption. Many of them end up being adopted by their foster parent, and being "managed" rather than rehabilitated.

Not every foster or rescuer will be equipped to work with dogs that suffer from behavior issues. It is imperative that you learn to recognize behavioral issues in dogs, and find a professional who can work with them.

Building Confidence

Building a dog's confidence is going to help him learn how to deal with stress, and is the best way to overcome fear-based behavioral issues. Dogs naturally are born with the ability to deal with stress and avoid conflict, and should be given an opportunity to practice these skills.

You can build your dog's confidence each time you

interact with him by requiring him to problem-solve and exert self-control. You can start confidence building when petting your dog. If your dog rolls over due to fear while you are petting him, stop. Petting him while he is fearful only reinforces the inappropriate behavior. By waiting until he is sitting or standing before petting him, you are showing him that his fear is inappropriate. You dog will have to problem-solve in order to figure out why you stopped and started petting him.

Your dog may have different fears such as being afraid of the vacuum, dishes rattling, kids playing or thunder. Do no react to any of these stimuli, but do praise your dog if he shows any confidence around them.

You can also build confidence by rewarding behavior you like. Praise your dog often for appropriate behavior. Feel free to give a pet or treat after verbal praise. In essence, you want your dog to feel he can do no wrong.

Hand-feed dogs with low confidence as often as possible. It may take a fearful dog a couple of days to begin offering behaviors in order to receive food.

When a dog with low confidence begins to try different things you should be thrilled. This means his confidence is growing and his problem-solving skills are improving. When he offers inappropriate behavior, just ignore or interrupt appropriately. One of the most common behaviors a dog will offer when his confidence increases is counter surfing.

To develop their skills, dogs must interact and socialize with dogs of different personalities and sizes. The more he interacts with dogs outside of his household, and the better he becomes at dog language, the more your dog's confidence will grow.

When dealing with symptoms that arise from a lack of confidence, you cannot just manage the symptoms. To be successful you have to get to the root of the issues, which is the confidence itself. Below are common behavioral issues, and how to remedy them.

Fear and Anxiety Issues

Fear and anxiety are *symptoms* of having a lack of confidence. Fear is an unpleasant feeling of anxiety or apprehension caused by the presence or anticipation of danger. A dog that feels fear will display rapid breathing, increased heart rate, a tucked tail, ears laid back, head lowered towards the ground and eyes averting away from the object of fear. Dogs can show more aggressive behavior when fearful, especially if their confidence is low. This behavior mimics Level 3 signals, and many humans see this as dominant or vicious behavior. Dogs that are fearful are unpredictable in their reactions to specific stimuli. A dog that is truly aggressive or vicious will be predictable in that he will always display aggression toward specific stimuli.

It is critical that you read a dog's entire body and use dog language when working with a dog who has behavioral issues. Communicating properly with your dog will help build trust between the two of you. You will not coddle the dog; it is also important you stay confident and non-confrontational.

As a rescuer, you will focus on building your dog's confidence, the underlying root of the issue. You will ignore the symptoms and not allow the dog to avoid its stressors. Once a dog's confidence is built up, many of the symptoms will dissipate.

When interacting with dogs that suffer from fear and anxiety you must keep a few rules in mind. First, you must control your own emotions about your dog. Focusing on the dog's past and what it may have gone through will keep you, and the dog, in the past. The dog may have been abused, mistreated or chained up, however, many dogs that have never been abused also suffer from these behavioral issues. Babying, coddling or reassuring him only reinforces his behavior and keeps him in the throes of anxiety. Be strong, confident and consistent so your dog has a true leader to cling to while improving.

Next, you will not allow your dog to avoid situations he views as stressful. If he has a fear of strangers coming into the home do not allow him hide under the bed or in his crate. You will not throw him to the wolves by forcing him to be petted by strangers, however he needs to stay in the vicinity, controlled by you. If you are afraid of something and never face it, you will remain afraid. Likewise, if you are forced to be constantly surrounded by your fear, you will shut down and never overcome the fear. There must be a balance between exposure and avoidance. Dogs are similar in that if we overwhelm them with something they fear, they will shut down. However, avoidance will not get them to the next step.

The final rule is committing to working with your dog until he overcomes his issue. You must ensure that everyone that comes in contact with him helps increase his confidence level and is consistently following the rules you put into place.

Fear of Doors

Many dogs are afraid to walk through doors. This is a behavior that you cannot ignore due to the need for the dog to go out or come in. When working on this behavior you must limit the dog's options by putting your dog on a leash and walking over a threshold with him. If your dog hesitates, keep moving or you will be rewarding the inappropriate behavior. If you move in a matter-of-fact way, you display to the dog there is nothing to fear. Do not coax him through by using a treat or reassuring words, and do not carry the dog. Once the dog is going through the door on a leash consistently without hesitation give him the option of doing it off lead, on his own. Remember to use a permission word each time the dog goes in or out of a door. Verbally praise for the good behavior.

Fear of Strangers

Dogs that have not been socialized with people on a regular basis may have a fear of strangers. This can cause a lot of issues when guests come to your home or when trying to take the dog to meet potential adopters. This behavior must be dealt with quickly so that the dog has the best chance of getting adopted.

People often resort to coddling and reassurance, or have the stranger give a treat to the dog so he will see them as friendly. Having a stranger give a treat to a dog that is frightened is not teaching the dog that strangers are good; it is only rewarding him for being afraid. Another mistake people make is they try to "talk a dog" into liking them by using "baby talk" and reaching out towards the dog with an extended hand. These techniques do not work when changing a dog's association with strangers.

If you have a fear of snakes, putting one in your lap is not going to change your association, even if I gave you a hundred dollar bill. If I place the snake across the room and give you a hundred dollars for just being in the same room, you could probably handle that. However, slowly, I am going to require you to move closer before earning the hundred dollars. Eventually, I may require you to stand next to the snake or even touch the snake but instead of a hundred dollars I am going to give you five hundred dollars. Would it be worth it to you? You may never love the snake but the anxiety you feel when you are around the snake will greatly diminish.

Similarly, with dogs, we must change the association with whatever is fearful; in this case, strangers. When working on this exercise it is imperative that you set up the dog to succeed by being prepared and controlling your immediate environment. I recommend you invite people to your home to work on this issue.

Before your guests arrive explain to them that their role is to ignore your dog completely. They are not allowed to look, touch or talk to him. Mix up different treats and place them in a pouch within easy reach; a treat bag that hangs on your pants is easiest. Be sure to use the shortest leash possible. You will limit your dog's options by not allowing him to flee into the other room or approach the stranger while exhibiting inappropriate behavior such as barking and lunging. When your accomplice arrives have someone other than yourself answer the door. If you are alone, instruct your guest to come in on his own. You will want to create enough space between you and your guest so that your dog feels semi-comfortable in the presence of the stranger. You know you are at the right distance when your dog gives you appropriate behavior such as ignoring the stranger. Do not to stop him from barking, lunging or growling, only ignore the inappropriate behavior and reward the appropriate behavior. Do not attempt to give him commands or stop him from offering different behaviors. When he chooses to offer a behavior that you would like to see again, verbally mark it and give him a yummy treat. When he exhibits the appropriate behavior consistently for a short amount of time, make a small movement towards the stranger. Your dog may bark, growl or lunge again, but you will ignore and give him an opportunity to use a different behavior. If he continues to display inappropriate behavior for a long period of time, move backwards until he is exhibiting the appropriate behavior again. However, this time you will not give him a treat. Instead, you will move forward once again. He can earn a treat when he is displaying appropriate behavior again. When you are close enough to your guest, allow your dog to greet your guest with permission. Your helper needs to ignore the dog at this time. Verbally mark and reward appropriate behavior such as sniffing, being quiet, or even ignoring the stranger. Your dog may give the stranger a sign that he is comfortable enough to pet, but you are responsible for giving your helper the okay to do so. Do not stop verbally praising your dog with a random treat. When he seems comfortable enough, let him off the leash and allow him to make the choice to stay or go. At this point in the exercise your dog may leave the room, but if he stays reward verbally with random treats.

Do this exercise many times with different helpers. Each time your dog may not be comfortable enough to approach, and you will not force him to do so. Get as close as you can while he is exhibiting appropriate behavior. Watch for signs of too much stress such as the inability to calm down no matter the distance, excessive panting or submissive urination. Some dogs can only handle short increments of training during stressful situations such as this.

When you move outside the home to work on this behavior take small steps. When in public you may not get to the point to where strangers can greet your dog but each time you are able to praise your dog for the appropriate behavior around strangers you are one step closer to changing his association.

As you progress through the steps of this exercise begin requiring your dog to show more confidence before earning the yummy treats.

Fear of Noises

Pots and pans clinging together, the vacuum cleaner running, plastic bags crumpling or thunder are just a few noises that dogs may fear. A dog that is afraid of noise was not necessarily abused by or with the items making the noise. The lack of confidence he suffers from prevents him from dealing with the stress they bring.

Noises occur on a regular basis and not controllable. Do not acknowledge the dog when he is exhibiting inappropriate behavior around these noises. Do not baby, coddle or reassure the dog. When you get appropriate behavior, acknowledge and reward.

Some situations may need to be managed unless you have assistance. Some dogs attempt to attack the vacuum instead of running from it. If your dog attacks from fear then you need to have a helper put him on leash and work the exercise as if the vacuum were a stranger coming into the house. Until you have a helper, you can isolate the dog somewhere safe until after you vacuum. This will only manage the issue, not solve it.

Thunderstorms and fireworks cause an immense amount of stress for many dogs. When a storm occurs while you are home take the opportunity to work on this behavior. This will help your dog self-soothe when you are not home during a storm. Again, do not baby, coddle or reassure. Act as though it is not storming. Do not allow the dog to avoid the situation by hiding under the bed, in his crate or in the closet by attaching a leash and keeping him beside you. Ignore inappropriate behavior and reward the appropriate behavior. CD's that produce the sound of thunder are available but cannot replicate the barometric pressure changes and rattling of windows; still, it will not hurt to play these quietly throughout the times you are home with your dog.

There are tools that can help your dog when dealing with stress such as thunderstorms, especially if you are unable to be home or work on the problem. I recommend the Thundershirt™ but only as a tool to assist your dog in getting through stressful moments. You still need to build your dog's confidence and not allow him to avoid situations.

Surface Anxiety

Some dogs have a problem with surfaces such as carpet, concrete, or hardwood floors. Often building confidence is not enough to get the dog over the fear so you have to deal with it specifically.

Your dog cannot remain afraid of your tiled kitchen floor, especially if the door to the backyard is located in the kitchen, or this is where you prefer to feed. Unlike the exercise that requires you to walk with your leashed dog over a threshold, you will not force your dog to walk on the surface he fears. Instead, you are going to take small steps to change his association with the floor.

To begin changing your dog's association with a surface, begin by using a longer leash than normal. Hook the leash to your dog, and allow him to stand on an adjacent surface (i.e.

the carpet outside the tiled kitchen). You will hold the leash, and stand on the "offending" surface. Do not pull the dog toward you. You will, however, encourage him to move onto the tile by clapping your hands, squatting and using the "come" command. When he takes one step onto the surface, verbally mark it and reward him with a treat. He is allowed to step back to safe ground after he has eaten his treat. Once he is offering one paw consistently, require your dog to place two paws on the surface before earning the reward. Do this until you are getting four paws and/or a few steps forward before rewarding. Each exercise can be done in as little as five minutes at a time. Do not move too quickly for your dog. Be sure you get each step consistently before requiring more behavior from him. If you observe your dog walking on the surface on his own, give praise and reward.

You can also encourage your dog to overcome his fear of surfaces by feeding him on that particular surface. Once you give your dog permission to eat move away from the bowl and ignore him. Give him twenty minutes to eat. When the allotted time is up, pick up the bowl. It may take a couple of feedings before your dog realizes that he has to step onto the surface to eat. To start, place the bowl just inside the room with the surface. It should only be in far enough to where your dog has to place at least two paws on the surface to eat. When he is comfortable with that, move it farther into the room and require your dog to place all four paws on the surface. Eventually, move it into the room far enough to where your dog has to take a couple of steps before reaching the bowl and so on until it is no longer an issue.

Separation Anxiety

Separation anxiety is another symptom associated with a lack of confidence. Most often the anxiety is not bad enough to require medication or management when the dog is left alone, and building confidence should remedy the problem. However, dogs that suffer from severe separation anxiety and exhibit behavior that can be potentially dangerous require some sort of management (i.e. medication) during the confidence building stage.

There is a difference between a dog that is suffering from separation anxiety and one that is just unhappy about being left alone. Dogs that suffer from separation anxiety display other symptoms such as fear of strangers, noise phobia or surface anxiety. They will also show signs of stress upon the owner's return such as heavy panting, dilated pupils and rapid breathing. The dog may have defecated in the crate or attempted to chew or dig through the crate or wall. If your dog barks, whines, cries or eliminates in the crate but does not show any other signs of stress, he is just unhappy about being left alone. Most owners believe their dog suffers from separation anxiety because they claw at the door when left out of the bedroom at night. Dogs that claw at doors do so to communicate that they would like the barrier removed. If the owner removes this barrier, they are teaching their dog that their behavior works.

If your dog suffers from severe separation anxiety, and is harming himself when you are away, you must take precautions while you build his confidence. Finding a dog daycare where your dog can stay during the day can be helpful in that your dog can work on confidence-building here, and can be supervised throughout the day. Medications can lower the stress but may cause your dog to be lethargic and drowsy. Medications should be used sparingly if possible. Using natural medications can help your dog relax without the harsh side effects of prescription medications. Bach Flower Remedies offers natural products that help correct the emotional imbalances where negative emotions are replaced with positive emotions. The most popular remedy used for pets is Rescue Remedy. Rescue Remedy is a mixture of five different remedies to help promote calmness and relaxation. Rescue Remedy is designed to help deal with immediate issues but can be used for longer periods while working on building your dog's confidence. Bach products are available online.

Using a crate can be one of the safest places for your dog to be when left alone if your dog is not causing harm to himself. You can use a small room instead of a crate *if* your dog is not chewing up items that are off-limits or eliminating inappropriately.

Place your dog in his area five-ten minutes before you leave home. When you arrive home after being gone do not let your dog out or acknowledge him in any way unless he is exhibiting appropriate behavior. Be sure you give him permission when you let him out of his crate or room.

Submissive and Excitement Urination

Submissive urination can be frustrating for owners. Dogs of all ages can suffer from this symptom of a lack of confidence. Submissive urination can occur when walking towards a dog, talking to a dog or attempting to pet a dog. The best way to deal with submissive urination while you build up the confidence is to ignore your dog any time he exhibits fearful behaviors. Ignore and wait until he is showing less signs of fear and more signs of control. Do not punish the dog for urinating and do not encourage the dog's fear by giving him attention.

Excitement urination occurs due to a lack of self-control. The dog will not display signs of fear, but will instead display extreme excitement. Do not pay attention to your dog if he is overly excited; wait until he is exhibiting controlled excitement. Do not punish the dog or encourage the behaviors by acknowledging him.

Both behaviors can be eliminated over time. Some dogs will learn faster than others depending on the severity of the confidence issue or the uncontrollable excitement. Be patient and manage while teaching.

Resource Guarding

Resource guarding occurs when a dog becomes aggressive in response to either a human or other organism approaching a valued object. This valued object could be a toy, food on the floor, food in his food bowl or even you. Resource guarding is not a behavior that affects only dogs that have lived as strays. Dogs of all ages with normal backgrounds can exhibit this inappropriate behavior. Dogs protect objects from each other naturally. To determine whether your dog is resource guarding, first determine *why* the dog feels the need to guard an object. It is unacceptable for your dog to guard his bone from you because he does not see it as a privilege that you gave him. On the other hand it is acceptable for him to guard it from another dog in the house that keeps trying to take it from him. If you believe the dog has a right to guard something because someone is trying to obtain it inappropriately, then allow him to do so. However, if he is guarding something only because he does not want anyone else to have it, you must interrupt the behavior. You cannot be harsh when dealing with this behavior. You must be confident and you must have established the leadership role in a positive manner.

Guarding Food

Your dog is resource guarding his food if he growls when anyone or thing walks into the room while he is eating.

Growling at humans when eating is inappropriate. Teaching a dog that you control the food will help him to understand that he must count on you to if he wants to be fed. Begin hand-feeding and regular feeding exercises immediately.

For the first week, your dog must eat each meal by hand-feeding. You will require your dog to offer different behaviors to earn a bite of food from your hand. If your dog does not want to eat this way or shows any type of guarding behavior put the bowl away and feeding time is over. You may give your dog another chance if it is convenient for you to do so. Do not offer food as regular feeding at all the first week.

During the second week you will continue to hand-feed, but this time you will place the earned food into his bowl. Instead of offering a couple of pieces at a time, you will put a quarter of his meal into the bowl. This will allow you to get four offered behaviors from him. If at any time he starts to show guarding behavior with the food in the bowl, end the exercise.

For the third week, begin using the regular feeding exercises. Feed half a serving at a time, so his meal is divided into two portions. Once you give him permission to eat, stand close by and periodically toss a reward such as grilled chicken, hot dog or cheese into his bowl if he is not displaying any guarding behavior.

In the fourth week you will push him to allow you to touch him while he is eating before he receives an extra treat with his food. Start by touching him on the back. Immediately give praise and a treat if he allows you to touch him. Work on touching him for longer periods of time before giving him his verbal mark and treat. Do not do this more than six times during feeding at first, as you do not want to cause the dog to revert back to guarding.

If you feel you need to interrupt at any time place your dog on a long leash before you feed, this way if you need to interrupt you can pick up the leash at a distance and walk the dog away from the bowl. Do not reach for the bowl directly until you are confident the dog will not physically harm you. Change the feeding location periodically so your dog does not begin to guard an area.

As an exception, if you are unable to work on your dog's behavior during the first month exercises, isolate him in his crate or in a room while he eats. You will still require him to do the appropriate behavior for regular feeding.

If you are uncomfortable working on this exercise you should find a professional trainer in your area for assistance.

Guarding Humans

I see this behavior occur mostly with small dogs that are sitting in their owner's laps. No matter how small the dog is, this is inappropriate and can cause serious issues between family members. Luckily, this is an easy behavior to eliminate.

Your dog should not be in your lap or on the furniture unless given permission. If permission has been given and the dog is sitting nicely with the owner but then growls, snaps or barks when another human or dog attempts to come close, then the invitation must be revoked. Your dog needs to understand that growling at anyone or another dog while with the owner is unacceptable. If your dog does this, gently move him to the floor and say nothing. You do not need to scream, yell, or scold the dog. Putting him in the floor when he exhibits this guarding behavior will communicate to him that you find the behavior unacceptable. If he turns around and jumps right back up, put him back on the floor. If he attempts it two more times without permission he goes to a time-out. Do not invite him back up with you for at least thirty minutes after the incident.

When your dog exhibits good behavior when in your lap be sure to praise him. If you find that you are placing the dog in the floor for inappropriate behavior more than you are praising, then eliminate the furniture or lap for a couple of weeks to communicate your expectations and your leadership to your dog.

Guarding Furniture

Guarding furniture is an inappropriate behavior and must be interrupted. The same technique used above is applied to this guarding behavior. Each time the dog attempts to guard the furniture, remove him immediately. Gently pull him by the side of the collar and remove him. If you do not feel safe grabbing him by the collar then place a leash on him before you invite him up on the furniture so you can use the leash to pull him off. Either way, do it gently with no emotion and no words. It is preferred that the person he growls at is the same one that removes him.

Guarding Dog Bed

If your dog guards his own dog bed from humans or other dogs, he needs to be interrupted. You may use the leash technique to remove him from the bed for a thirty-second time-out, or remove the bed from underneath him. You must do what you are comfortable with. Praise your dog when he is not guarding his bed.

Touching

Many dogs have an aversion of being held or touched, especially if they have never received any positive associations with it. If owners do not work diligently on getting their dog used to being handled, problems will arise.

Most dogs do not mind being petted on the back, the neck and the head, but may be uncomfortable when touched on the paws or ears. Most owners never touch their dog's paws unless they are trying to trim nails. Nail trims can be associated with pain if the dog's nails have ever been trimmed too short. You can avoid these issues by playing with your dog's paws from an early age during feeding, grooming and playtime. If you have a dog that is older and not comfortable with having his paws touched it is important to associate something positive with the touch.

Put together a mixture of high value treats. Sit in a quiet area with your dog leashed. Gently touch the top of his leg for a second before giving him a verbal mark and a treat. Do this several times before moving lower. If at any time he pulls away from you, say nothing and repeat until he is not pulling away. When you reach his paw only touch the top of it before rewarding. Do this several times, requiring him to allow you to touch his paw for longer each time before earning the reward. When you have reached this point you may begin to touch the paw in different areas or wrap your hand around it. Give him verbal praise and a treat if he allows you do this for a second.

You may need to do this over several days or weeks to get your dog used to being touched in areas that he is uncomfortable with. If your dog attempts to bite, I recommend using a muzzle or contacting a professional in your area for assistance.

Human Aggression

Real human aggression will typically not present itself in rescue environments because vicious dogs are often euthanized before being pulled.

Aggression in dogs is usually linked to an underlying problem with fear. Dealing with the lack of confidence and associating positive rewards with humans will help treat this behavior problem.

The severity of your dog's fear will determine if you should work on this problem alone. If your dog is showing fear but avoiding humans, then you can use the "fear of strangers" technique mentioned earlier in this chapter. If your dog is exhibiting aggression from fear, and instigates aggression toward humans, you should contact a professional trainer in your area that is experienced in using positive methods. If your dog has ever bitten anyone you must seek professional help. Once a dog bites there is no guarantee that you alone can solve the issue and trust the dog. Biting relieves the stress the dog is feeling, causing him to do it faster and more often when stressed. Management is key, as you must be diligent about controlling your environment and dog to keep humans safe.

Do not use harsh techniques when working on this behavior, as they will only make the fear worse.

Some dogs suffer from fear and real aggression due to neurological or physical issues. Always have your veterinarian give your dog a complete physical with blood work. Be sure your vet does a full thyroid panel as well. Work with a veterinarian that has experience in aggression due to physical ailments or neurological problems.

Bullying

Dogs bully other dogs during playtime, social interaction, and greeting. Dogs that bully will try to establish leadership in an inappropriate, overbearing manner. Dogs become bullies because they lack the confidence to handle another dog *if* the other dog becomes dominant. The dog thinks with a, "I will get you before you get me" mentality.

Dogs that bully are not necessarily dominant. Please note that "bully" breeds (i.e. pit bulls, bull terriers, etc.) are not the only ones who are bullies, and not all of them display this behavior.

Dealing with a dog that is a bully to others must be done carefully. When he is showing inappropriate behavior such as holding a dog down that wants to get up, you cannot display emotion or scream and yell. Your arousal will only intensify the behavior, which can cause a fight between the dogs.

Calmly use "that's enough" as your command to a dog that is being a bully or displaying inappropriate behaviors. If the verbal command does not work, use a split-up technique. Follow through with time-outs if necessary. Continue to work on your dog's confidence level.

Excessive Mounting

Though mounting seems like an inappropriate behavior to humans, mounting is natural for dogs to do to one another. There are several different reasons dogs mount one another, and not all instances should be interrupted.

Not all mounting is done for sexual or reproductive purposes. Sexual mounting is slow and purposeful; the dog is typically positioned on the backside or flank area of another dog. When male dogs hump you may see a penis extension. Both male and female dogs may exhibit air humping after the dismount. Sexual mounting should be interrupted in instances when there is a possibility of conception, when a dog has hip or back problems, when there is a significant size difference between two dogs, or when one dog is constantly fixated on another dog, making it difficult for the mounted dog to go about normal functions.

The second type of mounting is arousal mounting and is done very quickly during excited play. This mount should not be interrupted as it occurs too quickly.

The final type of mounting is dominant mounting. This mount may not include humping. Dominant mounting can occur anywhere on the body of another dog, and is only interrupted if the mounting dog is turning into a bully. Both arousal and dominant mounting can turn into sexual mounting.

Excessive mounting occurs when the mounting dog follows another dog around and is constantly trying to mount. This should be interrupted with a verbal, a split-up, then a time-out if necessary.

Inner-Pack Aggression

Inner-pack aggression occurs often between a rescuer's foster and own dogs. I also see it occur between dogs that have lived together for years.

An occasional fight between housemates does not constitute inner-pack aggression; this is natural and will occur. Inner-pack aggression occurs when dogs consistently fight over territory, objects, and attention. These dogs will have a natural dislike for one another and may or may not be able to live together harmoniously. Dogs that have inner-pack aggression are not necessarily bad dogs and can probably live with the right dog without incident. If a dog displays aggression toward all dogs, the issue is dog aggression and not inner-pack aggression.

There is no guarantee that two dogs that suffer from this can learn to live together. However, through consistency and follow through, it is possible the issue can be improved.

Management is crucial while dealing with this behavior but it is not a solution. To believe you can have two dogs with inner-pack aggression live together by staying separated is unrealistic. It is unfair for dogs to be isolated from a pack for the duration of a day. I encourage you to never attempt to keep two dogs that will not get along. It is fairer to choose one of the dogs and rehome the other into an environment where he can live harmoniously.

I recommend utilizing a professional in your area that has experience in dealing with inner-pack aggression. Success does not occur in 100% of these cases, and the professional needs to be upfront and honest with you about expectations. The training should occur in the home with the family and not in a board and train environment.

CHAPTER 11
BEING IN PUBLIC AND EXTRA ACTIVITIES

Dogs will encounter many situations outside of the home while either in foster care or their forever homes. Many dogs in rescue have had negative associations with the outside world and may need some counter-conditioning to have a better chance of being adopted.

The world today is much different for dogs than it was twenty years ago. Almost every city has a dog park or some public place that accepts dogs. Even some hospitals and nursing homes are seeing the value of having pets visit. While it is great communities are accepting pets as an integral part of families, these communities are placing a lot of responsibility on owners to have well-mannered dogs.

Though it is impossible to train a dog for every situation he will encounter, you can give him the foundational skills, socialization and confidence building he needs to succeed while in public. Taking your dog in public is a great way for your rescue dog and your own dogs to practice socialization skills and other training.

Preparing Your Foster for Public Adoption Events

Many rescue organizations have established adoption

events where they are able to showcase their available dogs. To be successful, the dogs should have manners and self-control. Adoption events are also a great way to give your foster dog some training to improve his skills. Many rescuers who work adoption events allow the dogs to be rewarded for poor behavior such as pulling, lunging, barking and jumping. It is imperative that you stay consistent during these times to ensure success for your foster dog.

A dog kept in a shelter or isolated in a foster home will not be able to exhibit self-control and confidence during adoption events. A well-mannered dog will get more attention than a cute, ill-mannered dog.

Working on stationary exercises will help your foster dog become acclimated to being in public. Use dog parks, outdoor cafés, pet stores, playgrounds and other outdoor events in your community to practice. Do not overwhelm your dog by starting somewhere too busy. As the rescuer, you must be good at communicating to people that they are not allowed to give attention to your dog while in training unless given permission by you. The more places you can use and the more times you are successful the faster the dog will learn that expectations in public are the same as at home.

Dog Parks

Dog parks have many pros and cons. As an owner or rescuer, you must be aware of each so you can make the appropriate decision for your dog or foster dog. I recommend you visit your local dog park alone before taking your dogs. While there, observe how owners are allowing their dogs to behave. See if they are properly teaching their dogs to enhance their dog language skills, or if they are improperly disciplining dogs who are exhibiting proper dog language skills.

Dog parks allow your dog to socialize with dogs with different temperaments. Your dog will also benefit from the safety of a play area and the socialization with new people.

Cons include: lack of education of owners on dog communication and interaction and lack of sanitation.

Dog Daycare

Foster dogs can benefit greatly from a good dog daycare facility. Utilizing such a facility can also help relieve you of some of the training that goes into a foster dog.

As the founder and owner of one of the first dog daycares in Middle Tennessee, and consultant for many others, I cannot stress enough the importance of staff training and education. Successful daycares strive for training, education and safety of their dogs. I have seen daycares without proper training cause undue harm to many dogs.

When looking for a daycare that fits your needs and will benefit your dog, do your research. You should require complete answers to the following questions

What type of training does your staff receive?

A daycare staff should be trained in dog behavior, language, evaluation and supervision. An experienced professional should do the training, and each supervisor should go through testing to certify they are qualified. Ask to observe the supervisors with a group of dogs to ensure they are not rewarding inappropriate behavior such as jumping or barking. Supervisors should not be overly petting or playing with the dogs, and they should not allow any dogs to sit in their laps or upon tables.

What is the average ratio of dogs to supervisor?

The amount of dogs each supervisor can handle will depend on their experience. Average ratio should be one supervisor for every 10-15 dogs. Keep in mind that six rowdy dogs can be harder to handle than twelve laid back dogs. Ask to watch the supervisors on their busiest day.

How many supervisors do they have and will your dog have the same supervisor each week?

Even if a facility has multiple supervisors rotating throughout the week, there should always be a daycare manager. This person will share pertinent information to supervisors regarding specific dogs. If possible, take your dog to daycare on days when he can have the same supervisor.

How do you evaluate new dogs?

The evaluation process is critical to a successful daycare. New dogs should never be placed in an established playgroup before being evaluated, and an experienced supervisor should evaluate them. Dogs being evaluated should be tested with a minimum of three dogs with different personalities. A dog cannot be evaluated by just being looked at by the supervisor, a manager or with one other dog. Be sure the daycare gives a full report of the evaluation.

How do you break-up dog fights?

There are many techniques to interrupt a dogfight. You do not want the facility to use a spray bottle, water hose, pepper spray or a can full of pennies. These techniques are harsh, ineffective, and cause arousal, which will escalate a fight.

Do you give your dogs a break during the day?

When dogs get tired, they suffer from bad behavior. Most incidents and fights occur when dogs are tired. Breaks should occur in the middle of the day. Dogs should be placed in individual crates, runs or rooms for a minimum of one hour. The facility should not leave the responsibility upon the dogs to rest when they are tired.

Follow-up:

Always supervise a playgroup from a distance. It is not safe for you to be allowed into the playroom or yard when dogs are interacting. You may be able to supervise via a webcam or through a window.

Once you feel comfortable with a facility, give your dog a chance to visit a few times. Watch your dog's reaction when you drop off and when you pick up. If you find that your dog is exhibiting some behaviors he has not exhibited before, such as jumping or anxiety, then the facility may not be the correct one.

If you have a hard time finding a daycare for

socialization, reach out to other fosters and look for playtimes that can be set up for the dogs in foster. This will allow them to get the socialization they need and give you a chance to get to know other volunteers with the same passion as you.

Agility

Agility can be a fun extracurricular activity for you and your foster dog. It can build a bond, build confidence, teach self-control and get you both into shape. You do not have to compete in agility to enjoy it. Find a class that teaches agility for fun, using positive techniques. Classes should be small and run at a quick pace.

Therapy Dog

Many rescue dogs have the ability to become wonderful therapy dogs if given the chance.

You may notice your foster dog has a soft spot for children or the elderly. Taking your dog to different environments is important. You can use parking garages with elevators, home improvement stores with loud equipment and even retirement communities. Getting your dog used to different objects such as walkers, wheelchairs, and oxygen machines is critical. He will also need to get used to being petted in a rough fashion and should learn to not lick hands or faces.

For more information on helping your dog learn to be a therapy dog, search for local clubs that specialize in therapy work. They will have the information you will need to get him started on the right track.

CHAPTER 12
RESOURCES

I hope that this book has brought you much-needed education in order to help your foster and rescue dogs become confident, self-controlled, adoptable, and most importantly, happy. As a foster, I want you to focus on the dogs you can save, and on helping them become the dog they were intended to become. Below are some resources that will further your success with your foster dogs.

For a DVD that shows the exercises mentioned, contact Nikki at info@dogspeak101.com

Website: For the latest DogSpeak news, and to see how Nikki can help your rescue organization, visit www.dogspeak101.com

E-Training for Dogs: Bring Nikki's seminars, including "When Love Isn't Enough," to your home! www.e-trainingfordogs.com

Facebook: Get the latest news from DogSpeak! www.facebook.com/DogSpeak101

YouTube: Check out exclusive training videos! www.youtube.com/DogSpeak102

ABOUT THE AUTHOR

Nikki Ivey, professional Dog Trainer/Behavior Consultant is the owner and founder of DogSpeak™. She has been working with dogs and their owners since 1996. She has spread her wealth of knowledge to not only the general public but to the professional pet world as well. She loves to educate individually and in groups, wanting all pet owners and professionals to have a better understanding of dogs and to have the healthiest possible relationship with them.

Nikki has spent many years learning to truly understand the nature of dogs and their motivations. By letting go of the "dominant pack theory" method, she is allowed to be more in tune with dogs, and more effective using her own method of training known as DogSpeak™. Nikki uses positive methods with negative punishment such as time-outs, stopping playtime and taking away attention. She doesn't use any form of physical correction such as correction collars, shock devices or fake bites. This allows dogs to show their true personality, builds their confidence and always leaves them happy. It also ensures that children aren't being taught to be negative or physical with their dogs when teaching.

Nikki believes in clearly communicating with dogs, setting their expectations and giving them a confident leader. She teaches foundation skills to dogs such as self-control and problem solving. Once a solid foundation is in place, you can begin to build the walls of real life manners that go beyond the traditional obedience training of sit, stay, down, come and heel. With real life manners your dog will know how to respond in situations without having to be commanded by you; however, when you do need to command your dog, they respond quickly and enthusiastically.

Nikki also owned and operated the first dog daycare in Tennessee and has spent the last six years helping others build their successful daycares, either from the ground up or as an additive to an existing business. She trains staff members on dog behavior and interaction at daycares, veterinary clinics, and boarding facilities. Local rescue groups and shelters have started taking advantage of the knowledge and skill that Nikki has to help their foster parents understand the importance of foundation skills and being a confident, consistent leader.

In 2001, Nikki founded Tennessee Emergency Rescue and Recovery Association (TERRA), which uses K9s to locate missing persons and deceased individuals in water or land. She's not only a handler of a Human Remains Detection dog but also teaches other handlers to work their dog in HRD.

In addition to teaching, Nikki has also authored articles for various magazines and newspapers, is a handler for KlaasKids, Inc. and the National Center for Missing and Exploited Children and is a case manager for Polly Center.

In her spare time Nikki enjoys writing, and often incorporates her knowledge of search and rescue. Nikki's first

novel, *Callout*, is available online at any large bookstore.

Made in the USA
Monee, IL
28 February 2022